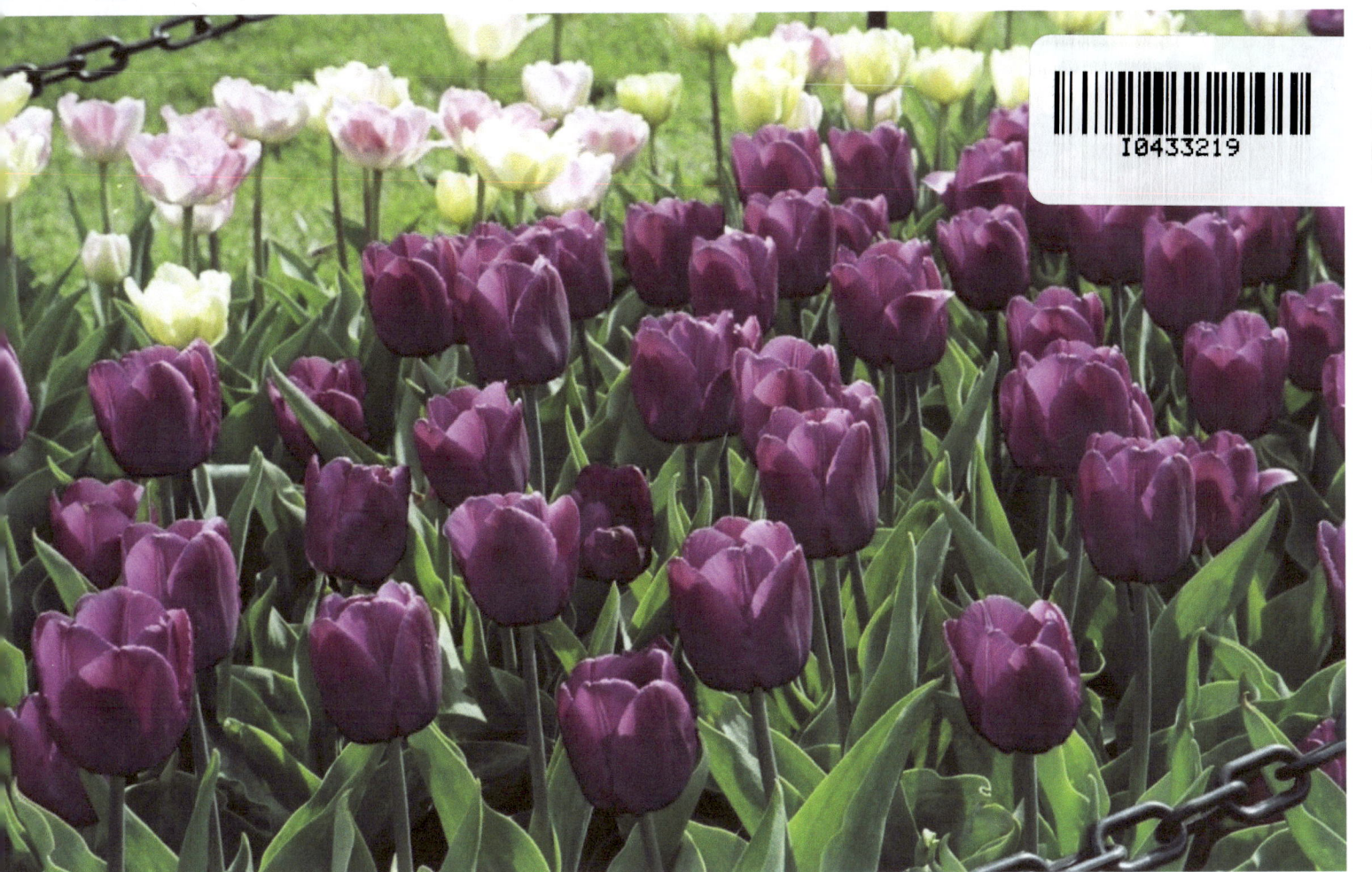

Poppa's Pics

Albany to the Adirondacks

By Benjamin Yates Brewster Jr., Anne Cammack Brewster, and James Burd Brewster
Photos by Benjamin Yates Brewster Jr.

J2B Publishing LLC, Pomfret, MD

J2B Publishing LLC
4251 Columbia Park Road
Pomfret, MD 20675
www.GladToDoIt.net

Text Copyright 2015 by: Benjamin Yates Brewster Jr.
                           Anne Cammack Brewster
                           James Burd Brewster

Photo Copyright 2015 by: Benjamin Yates Brewster Jr.

All photographs, unless otherwise noted, were taken by Benjamin Yates Brewster Jr.

ISBN: 978-1-941927-17-5

All rights reserved. No part of this publication may be reproduced, stored in a retrieval system, or transmitted in any form or by any means, electronic, mechanical, photocopying, recording, or otherwise, without prior written permission of the publisher. The only exception is brief quotations for reviews.

Cover Photo - After the Rain -Taken from the porch of Captain's Cabin after a typical summer afternoon thunder shower. I took it because rainbows are always stunningly beautiful and not that common.

Title Page Photo - Royal Tulips - A short walk from our State Street stoop is Washington Park and its beautiful tulip beds.

Introduction

Our family has lived in Albany, NY, and summered on Lake Champlain at Essex, NY, for over 50 years. These few photographs, selected from among many, reflect special personal moments.

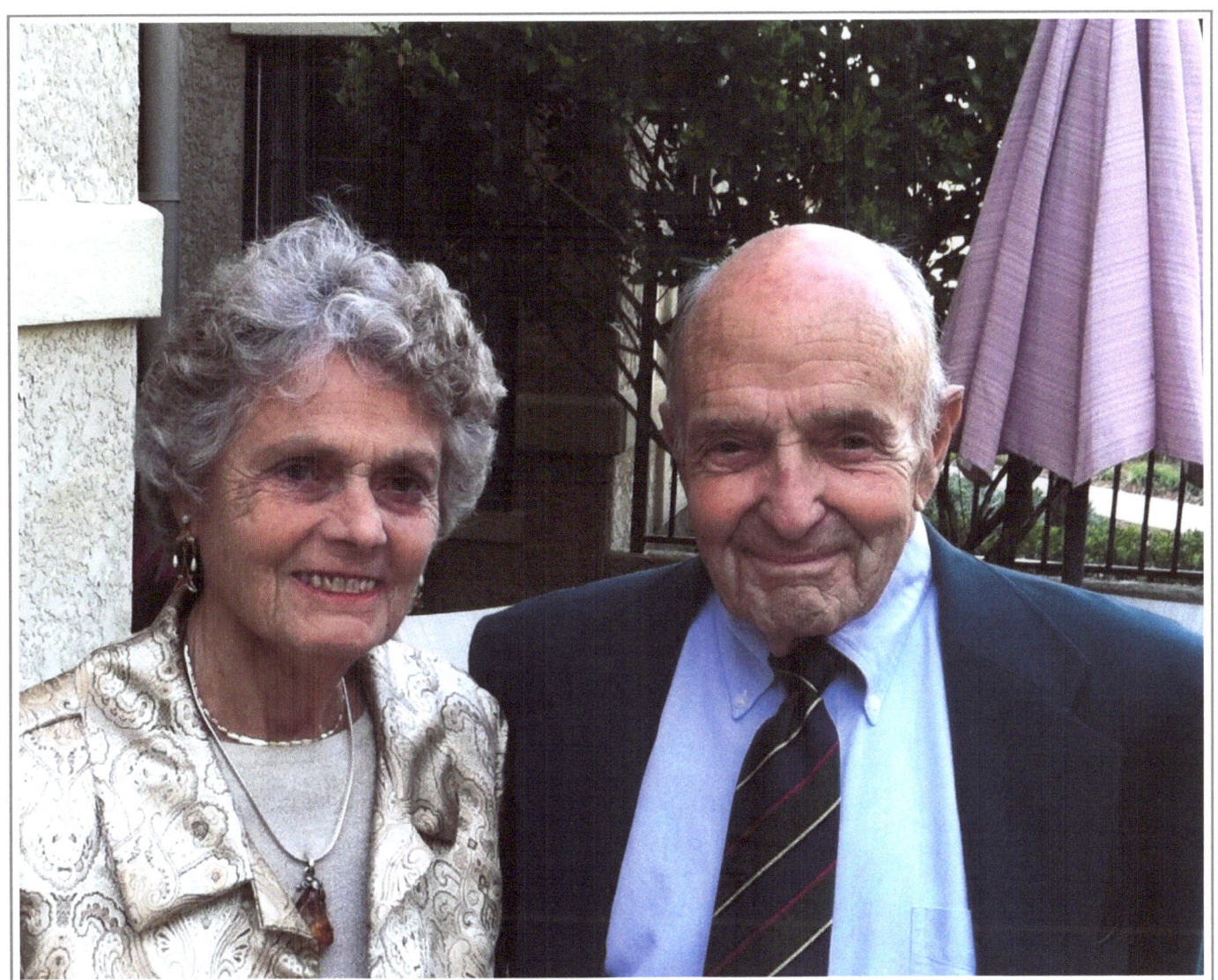

60 Years together
Anne Cammack Brewster and Benjamin Yates Brewster Jr.
Easter 2010 - St. Augustine, FL

Photo by James Burd Brewster

Albany, NY

Anne and I settled in Albany, NY, in 1956, two years after my naval discharge in 1954. Our first home was in the city limits at 24 Terrace Avenue. We moved the family to Slingerlands, an Albany suburb, in 1963 and lived there during the children's high school years. After Margaret, the last, left for college in 1979, Anne and I moved back into Albany to a 3-story State Street brownstone bordering Washington Park, where we were within walking distance of church and work. After a brief sojourn to St. Augustine, Fl, we moved to Beverwyck, a senior living community in Slingerlands, NY, where we now reside.

Anne and I have attended and supported All Saints Cathedral for almost 60 years.

I have been making pictures most of my life starting with drawing and watercolors in my teens and then with our first 35 mm camera, acquired while stationed in French Morocco with the US Navy. Except for ten years with Super Eight, I have chronicled our family and our travels on 35 mm. About twenty years ago I was encouraged to exhibit, which I have done each year since at the Adirondack Art Association gallery in Essex, NY.

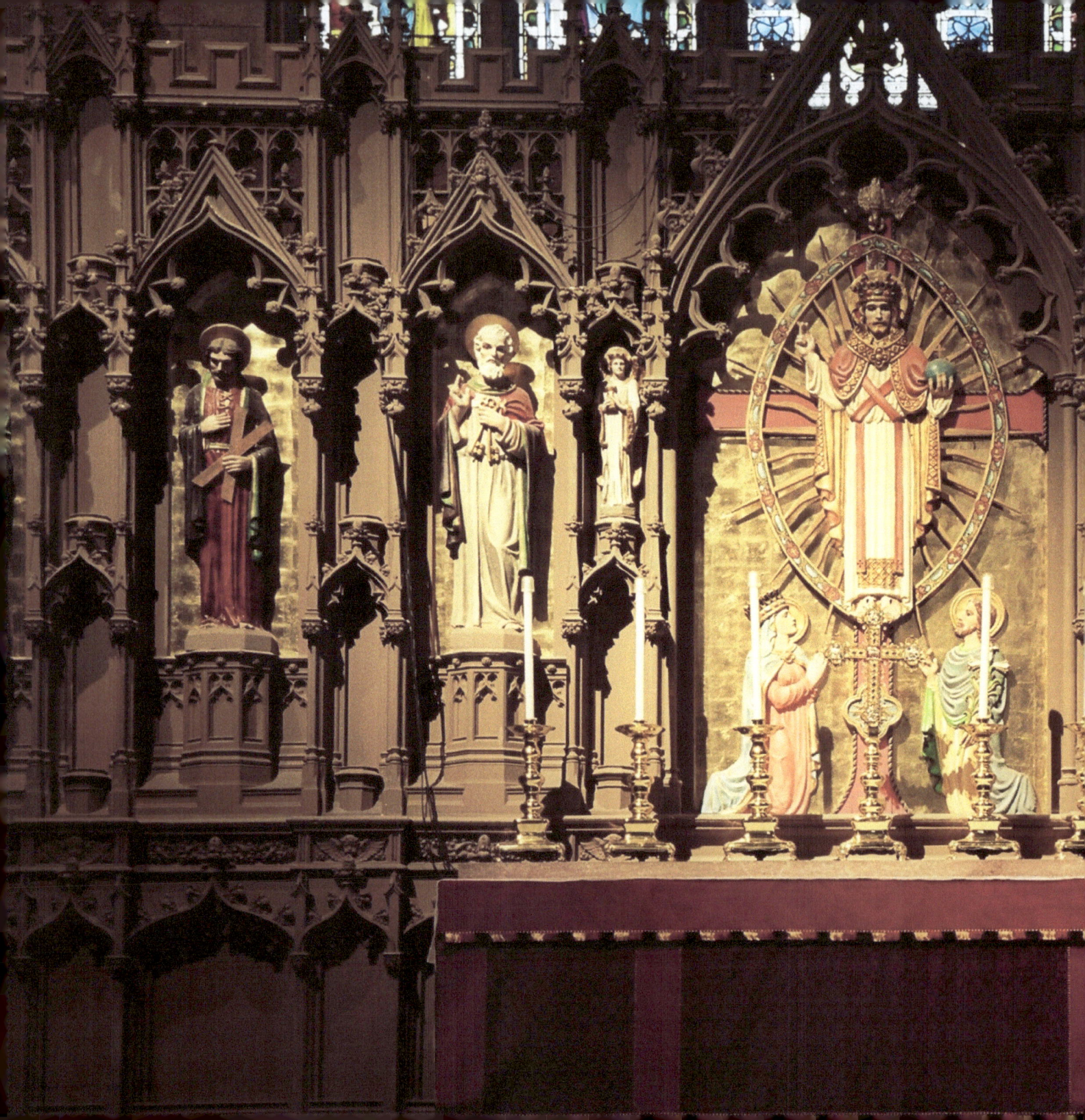

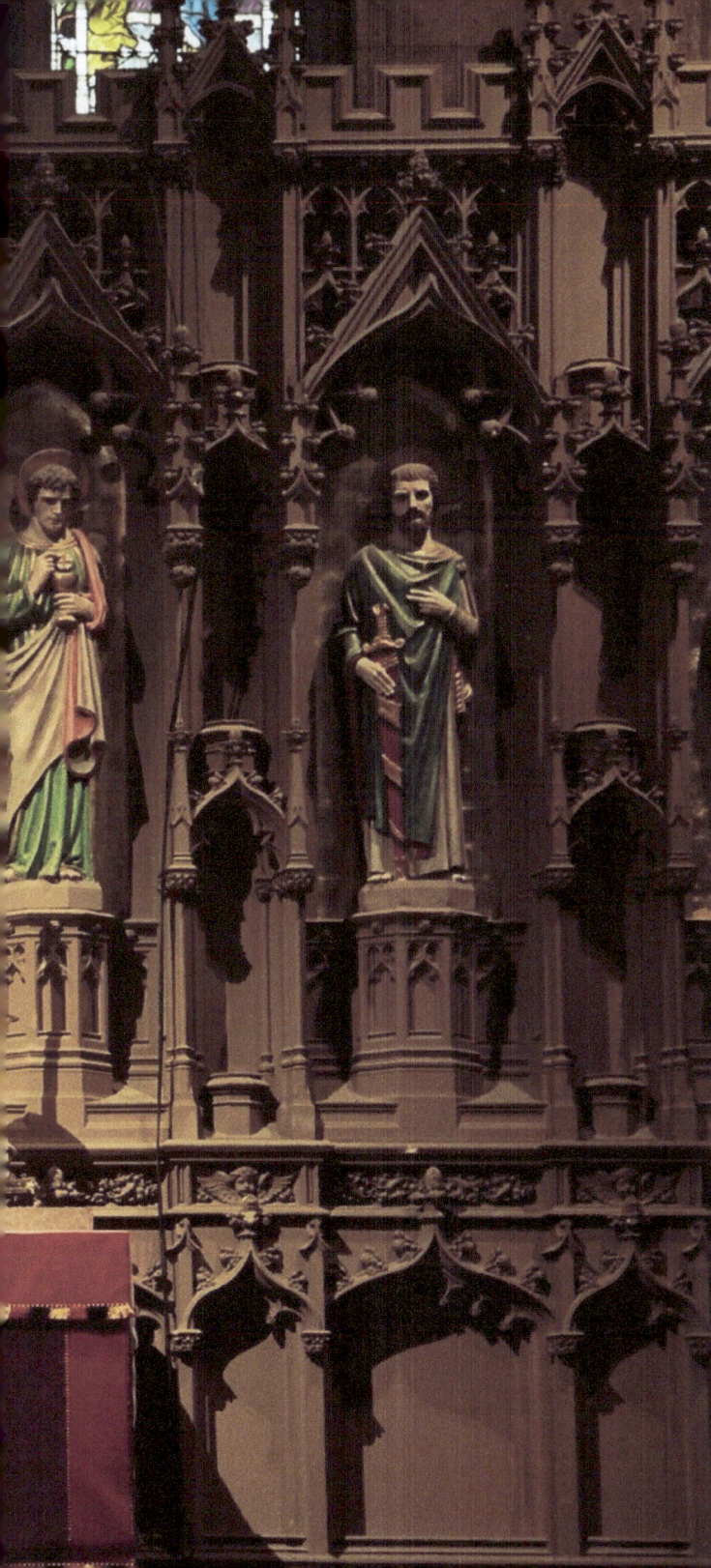

Cathedral of all Saints Altar and Reredos

Swan Street, Albany, NY

The cathedral has been our church since we first started attending in 1956, when we moved to Albany. All of our children were confirmed at All Saints.

It is also the central church of the Episcopal Diocese of Albany and the seat of its Bishop. The cathedral's cornerstone was laid in the summer of 1884.

The Reredos, the intricately carved screen behind the altar displaying statues of the saints, beautifully compliments the cathedral's stained glass windows, particularly the Great East Window above it which is one of the largest stained glass windows in America.

The cathedral is a marvelous acoustical space. Anne and I always enjoy listening to its spectacular organ and its noted men and boys choir.

Cathedral of All Saints South Transept

**Swan Street
Albany, NY**

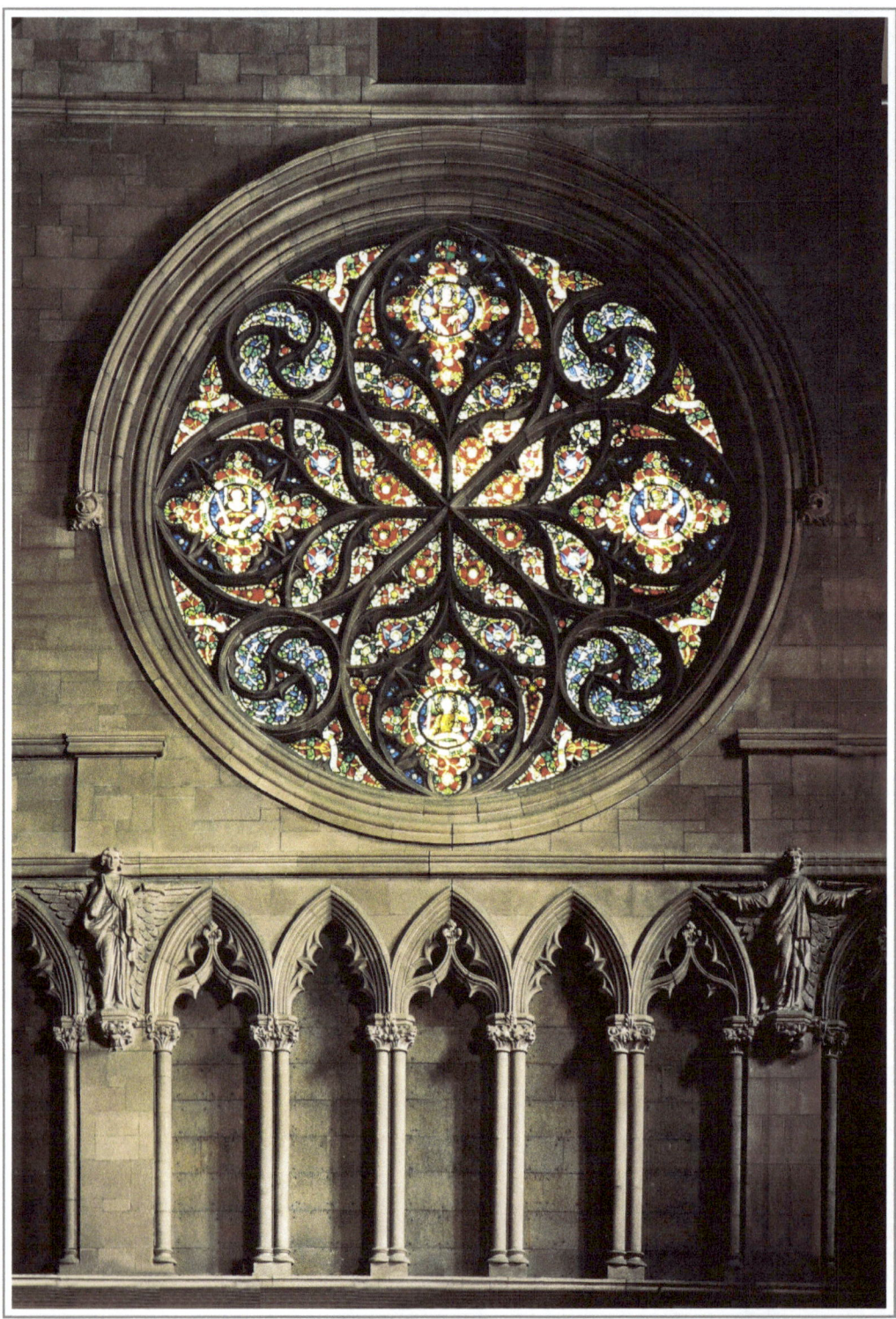

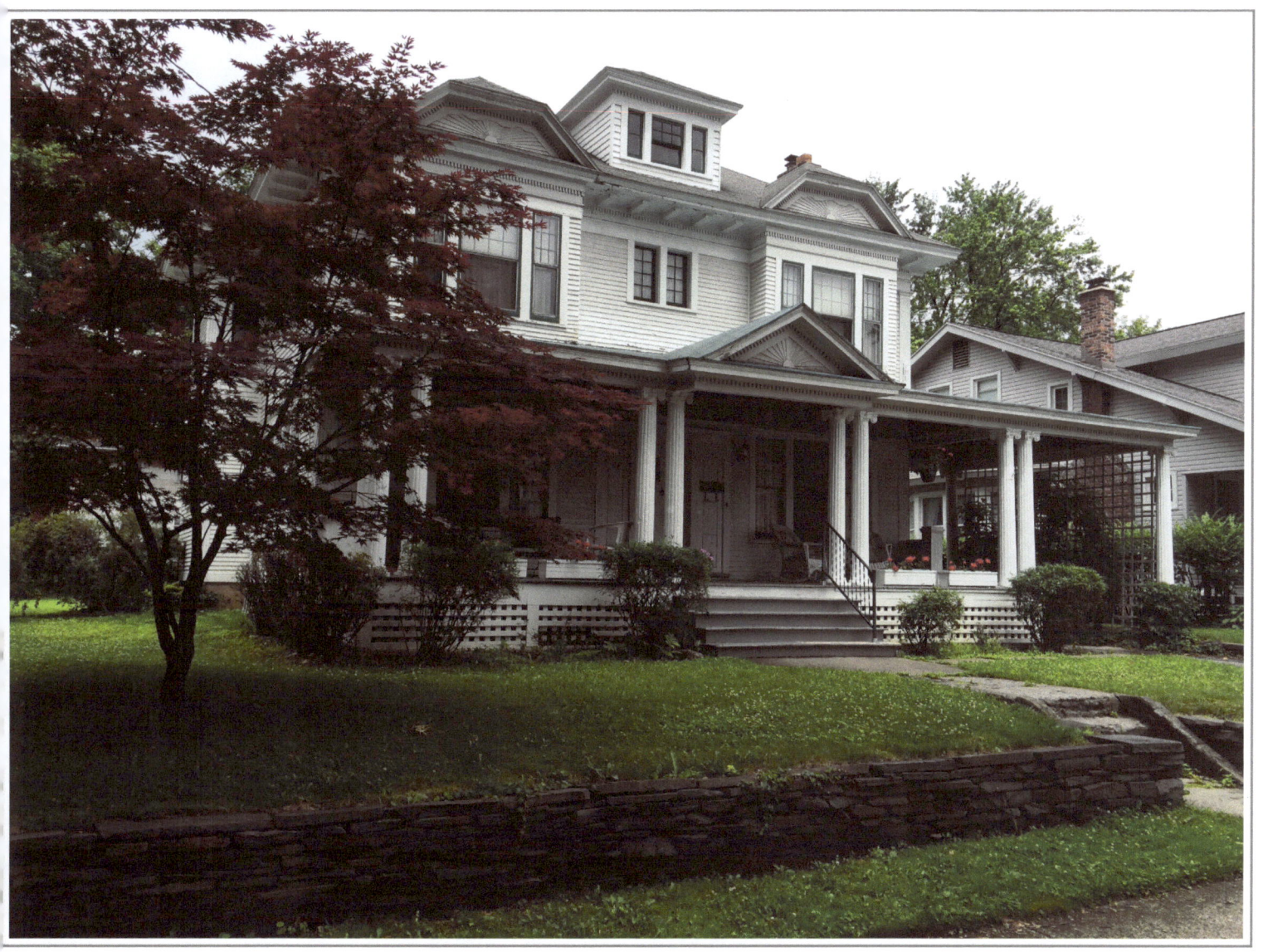

24 Terrace Ave, Albany, NY

Our family home from 1956 - 1963. We put in the dry stone retaining wall in 1962. It was a big house on a quiet street with enjoyable neighbors.

Photo by James Burd Brewster

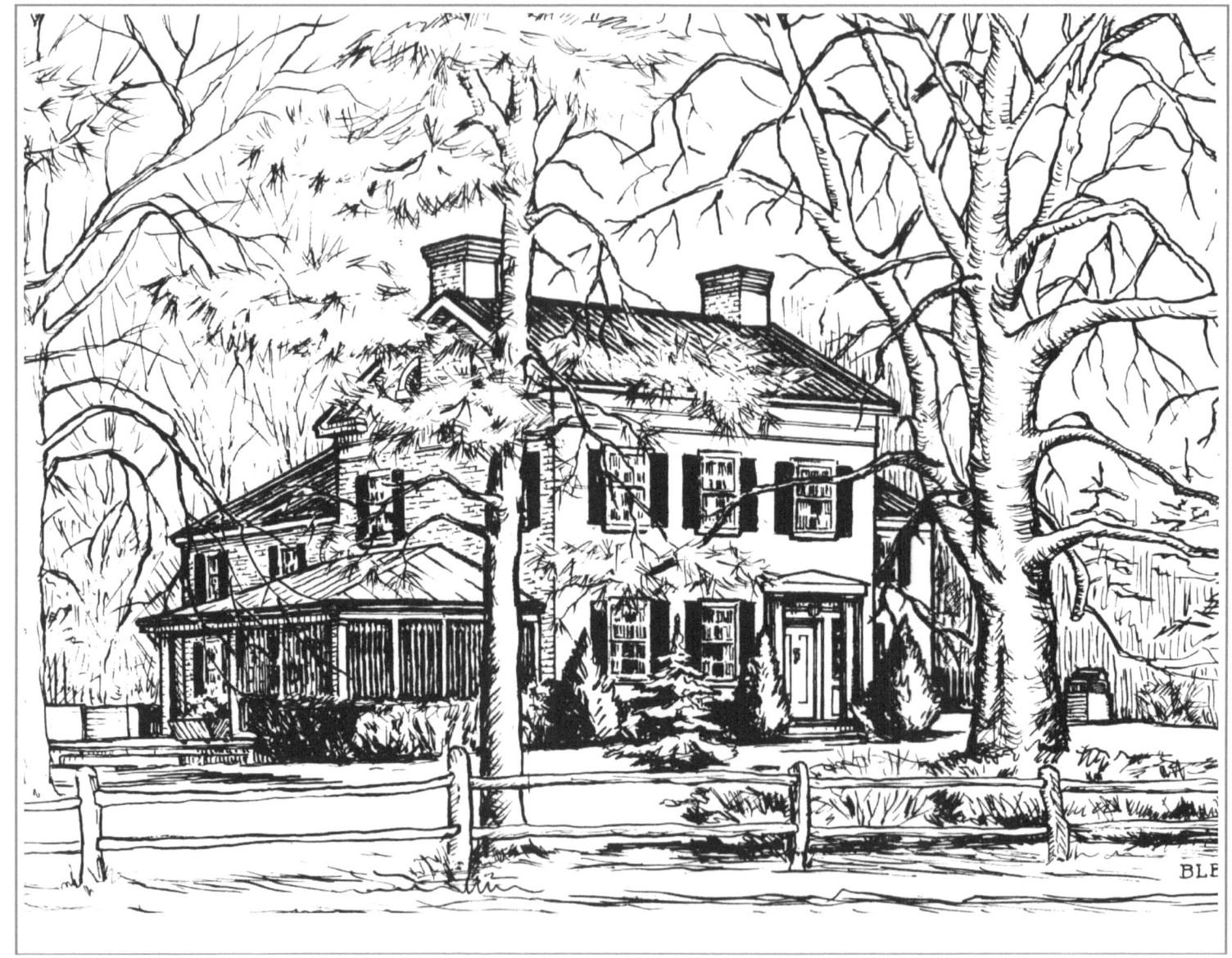

1719 New Scotland Road, Slingerlands, NY

Our family home from 1963 - 1979 in a suburb of Albany, NY. Built in 1841. A great place to raise a family.

Drawn by Barbara Boynton, a good friend and neighbor

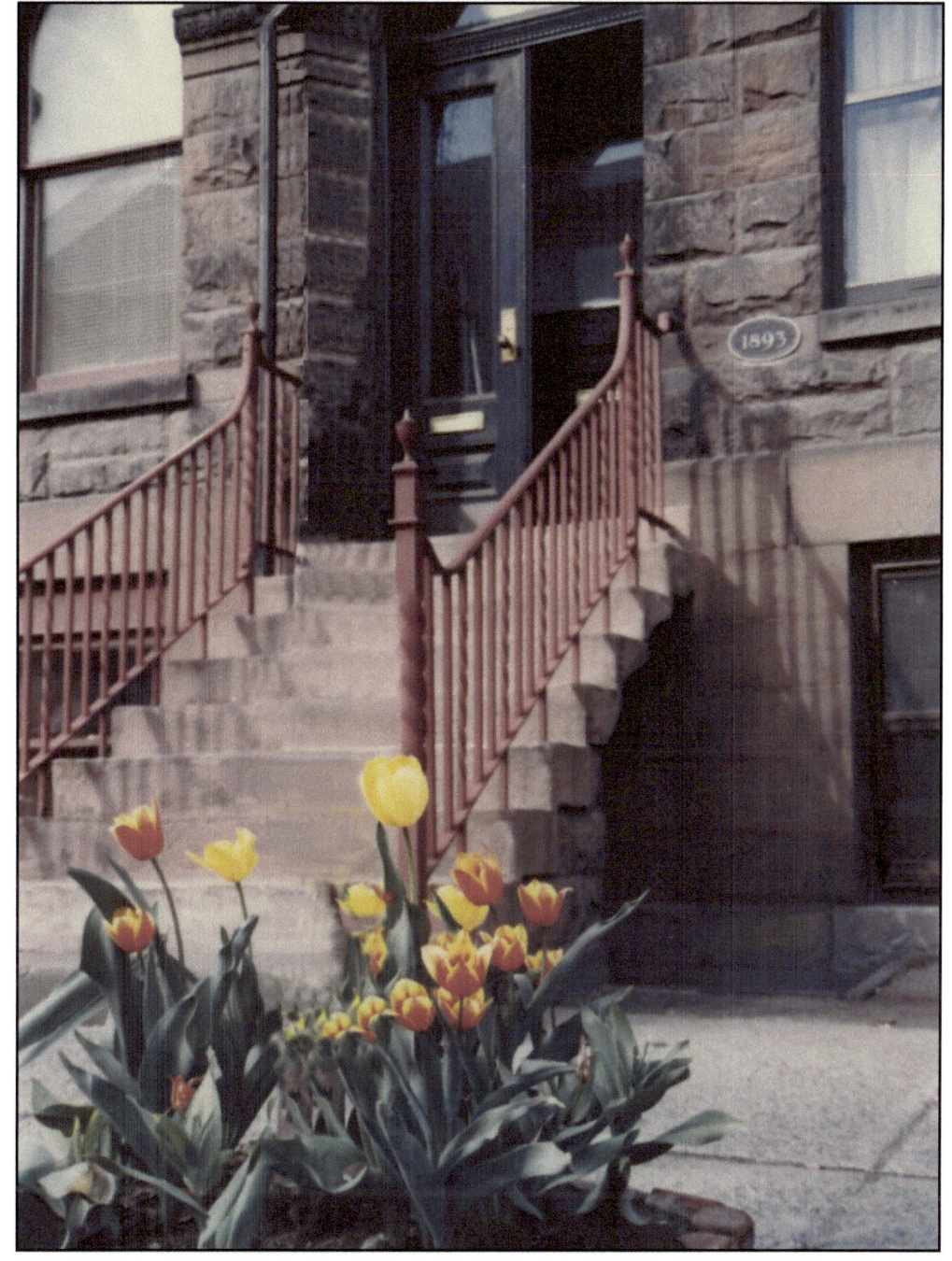

365 State Street, Albany, NY

Anne and I moved in across from Washington Park in 1979 and converted this three story brownstone from apartments back to its original one-family configuration.

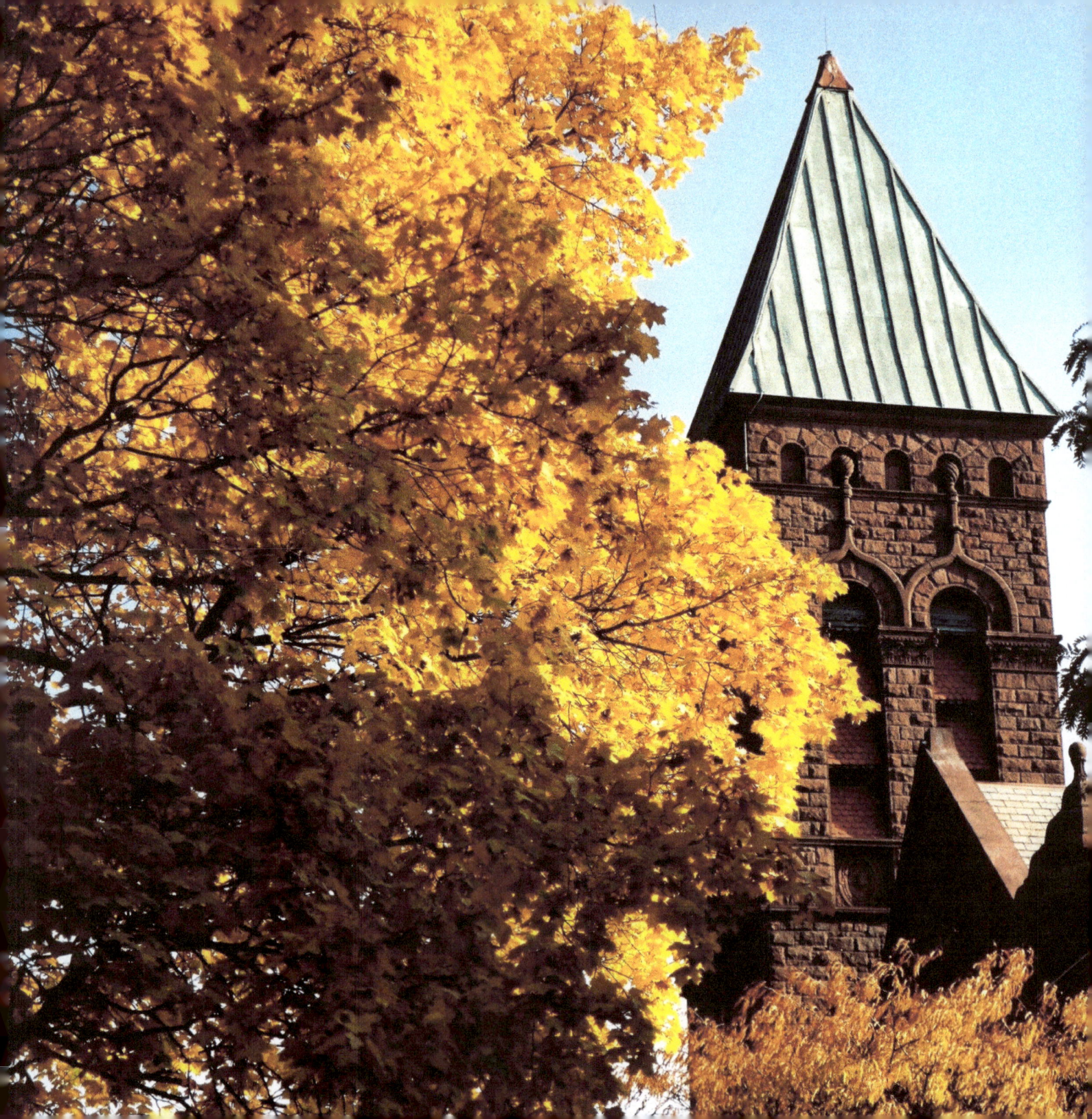

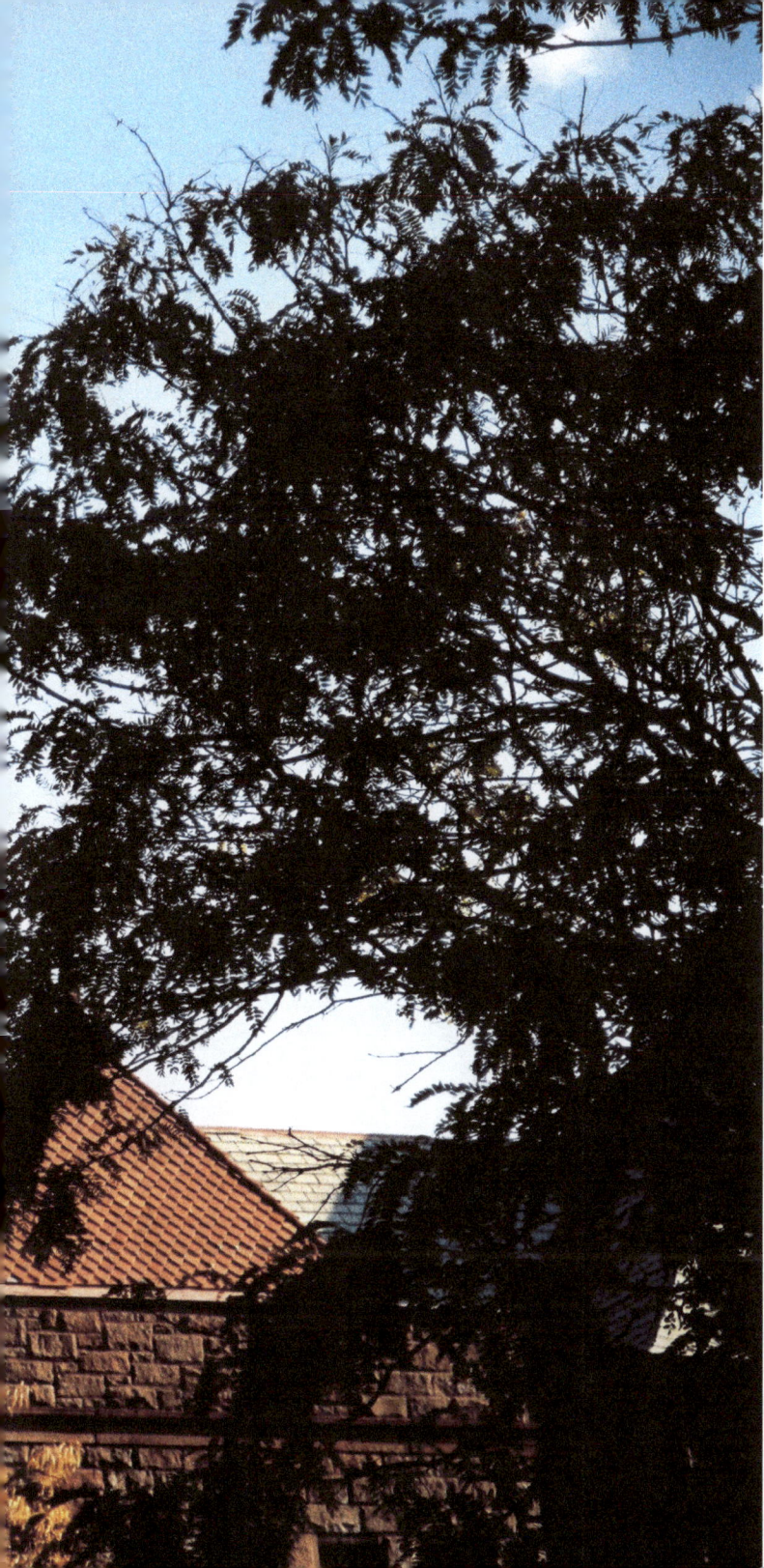

First Presbyterian Church, October

**State Street
Albany, NY**

Our brownstone faced this church across State Street. This photo was taken from the Washington Park side.

Playground

Washington Park
Albany, NY

It was a lovely October afternoon with the trees in high color. Snapping shots as I walked through the park, I came upon this gaily painted playground structure which suggested it was the bridge of a steamship or battleship. With the yellow background foliage, I couldn't resist.

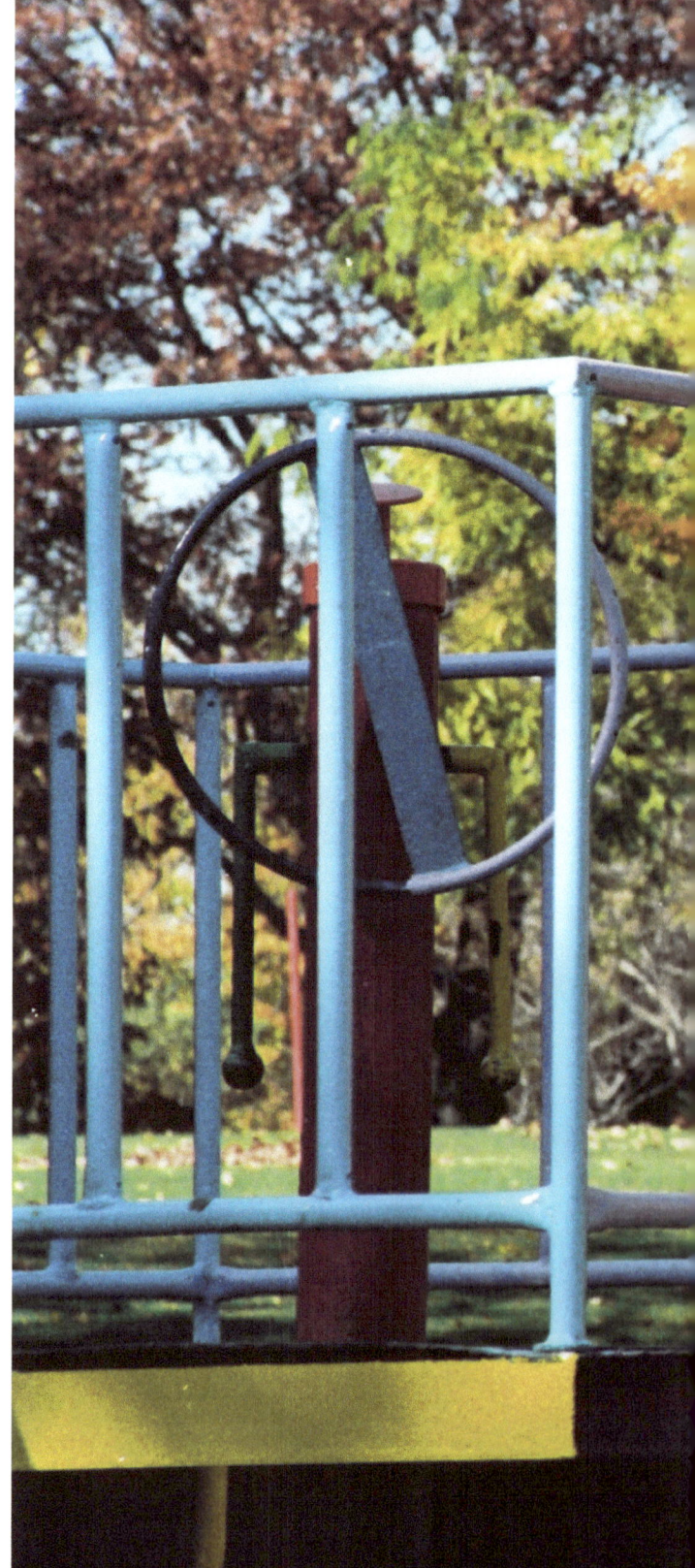

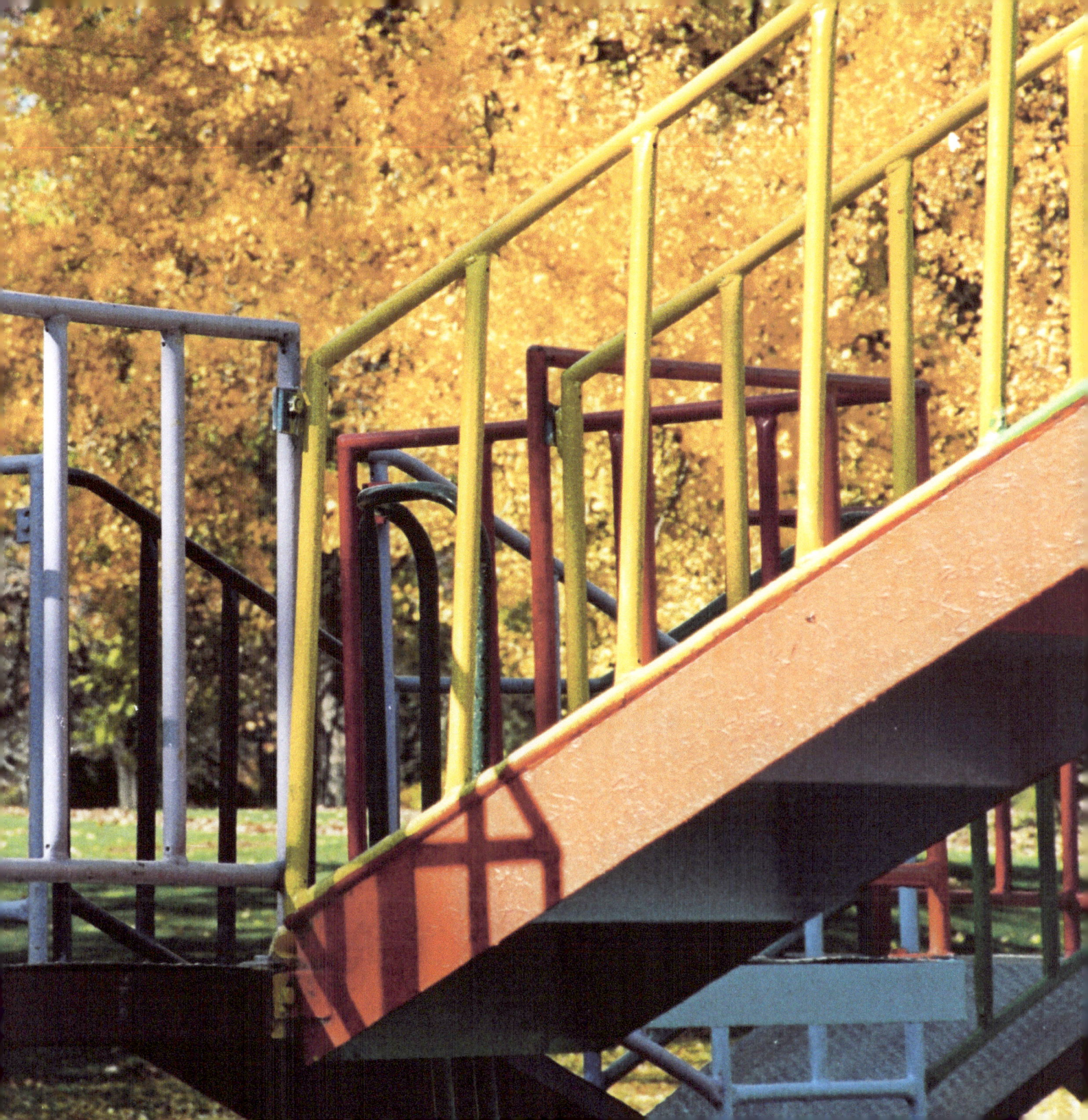

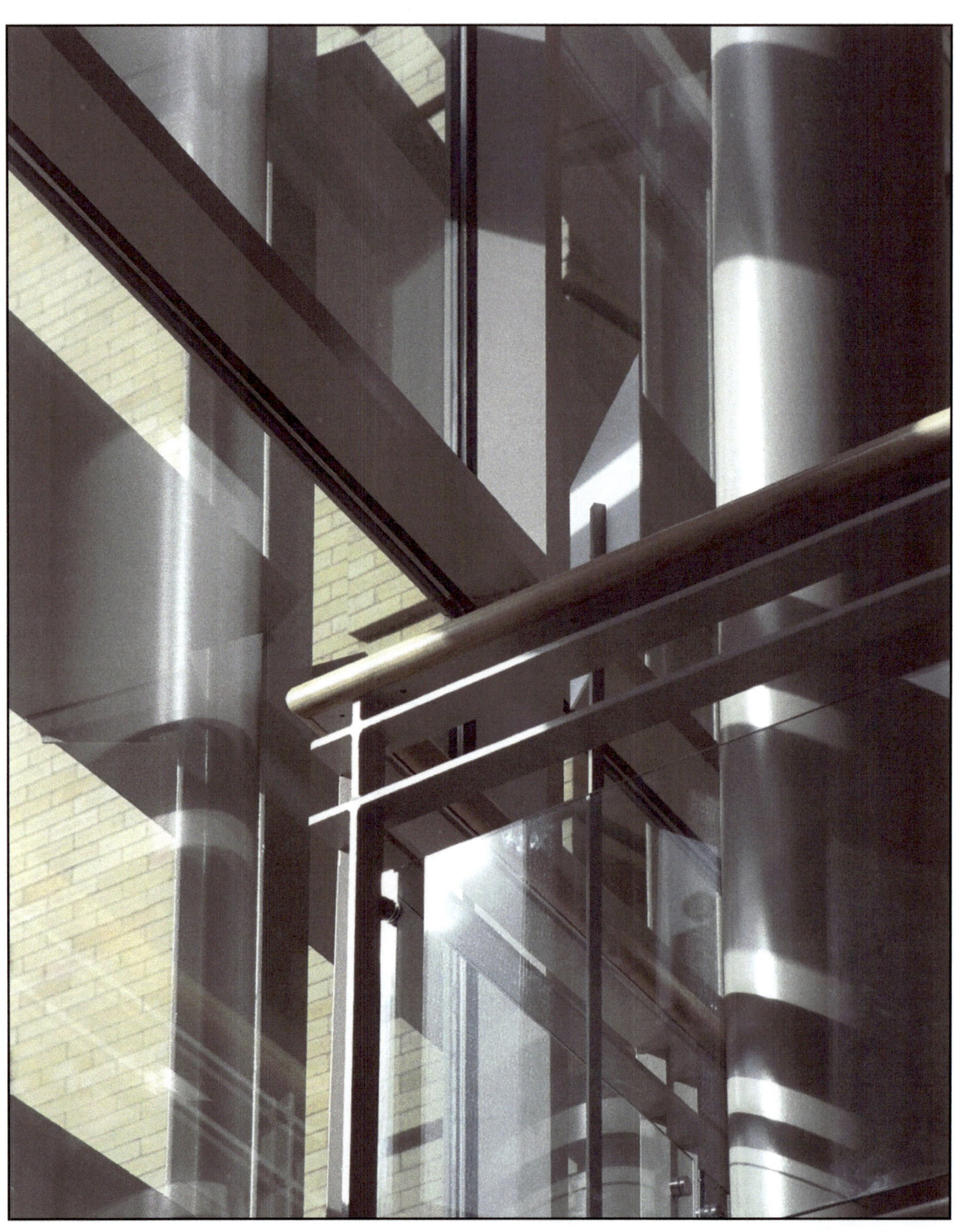

Albany Institute, 2001

Washington Avenue Albany, NY

Architecturally, Albany is a late 19th century city. These 21st century girders are within a sunlit atrium which welcomes the public to the Albany Institute of History and Art.

Standing in the new lobby of the institute after its renovation, I happened to look up and saw this irresistible subject.

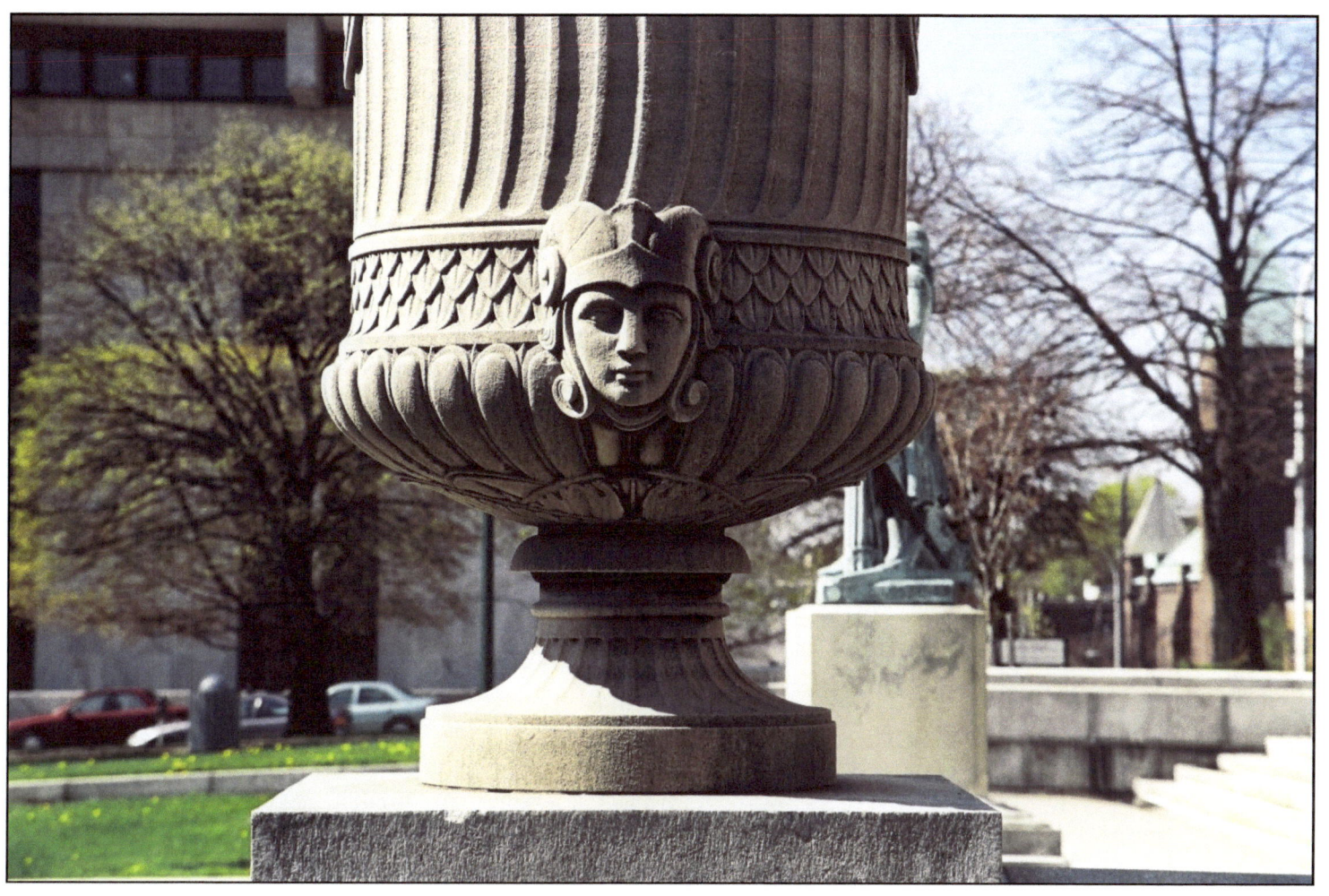

Statuary Urn
Capital Park, Albany, NY

I took a walk down State Street to the State Capital Building and came across this urn with the morning sunlight creating a shadow that perfectly bisected the face.

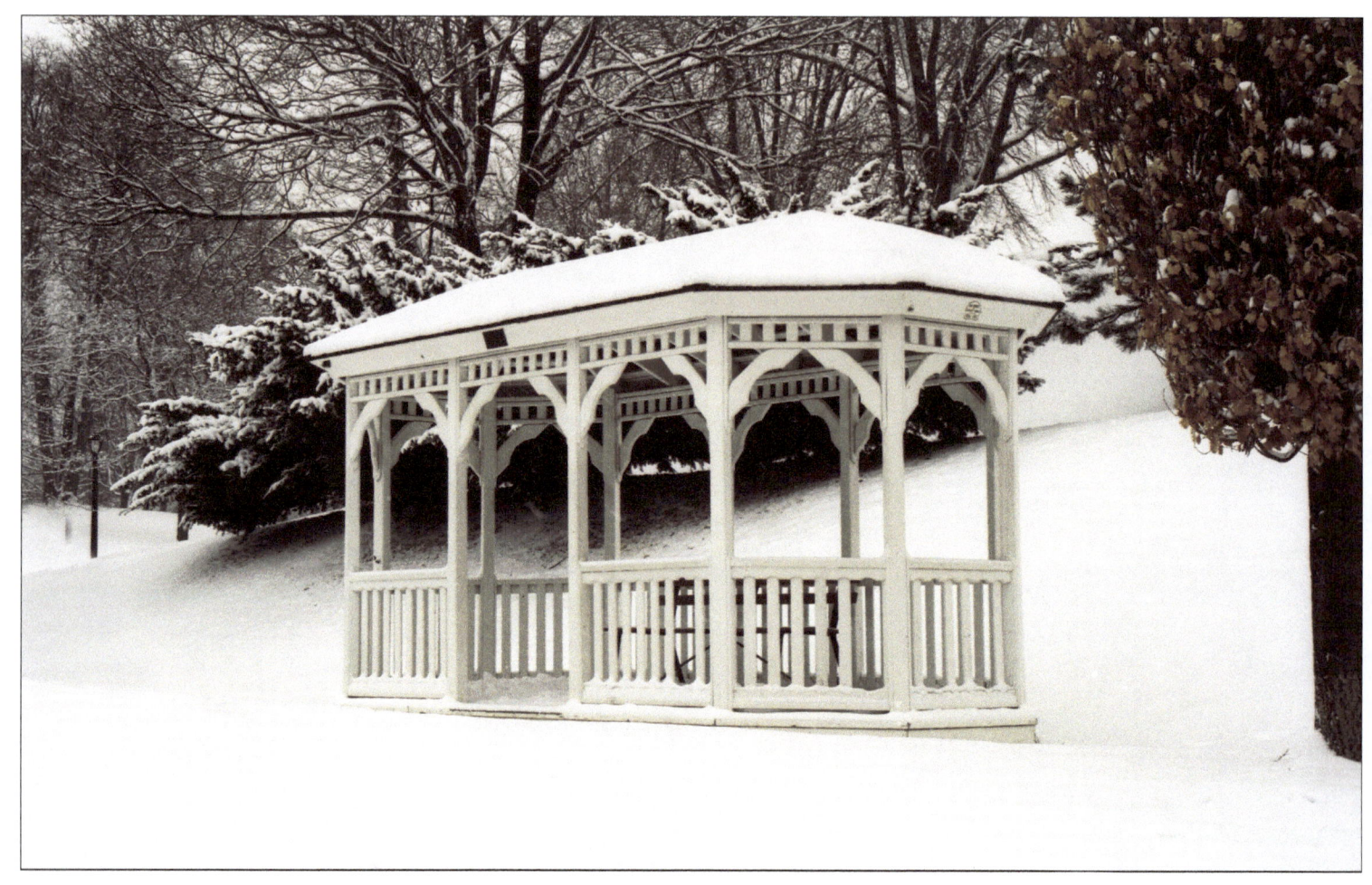

Park Gazebo, March
Washington Park, Albany, NY

This late winter shot in Washington Park was taken in the evening after an early March snow storm in 2006.

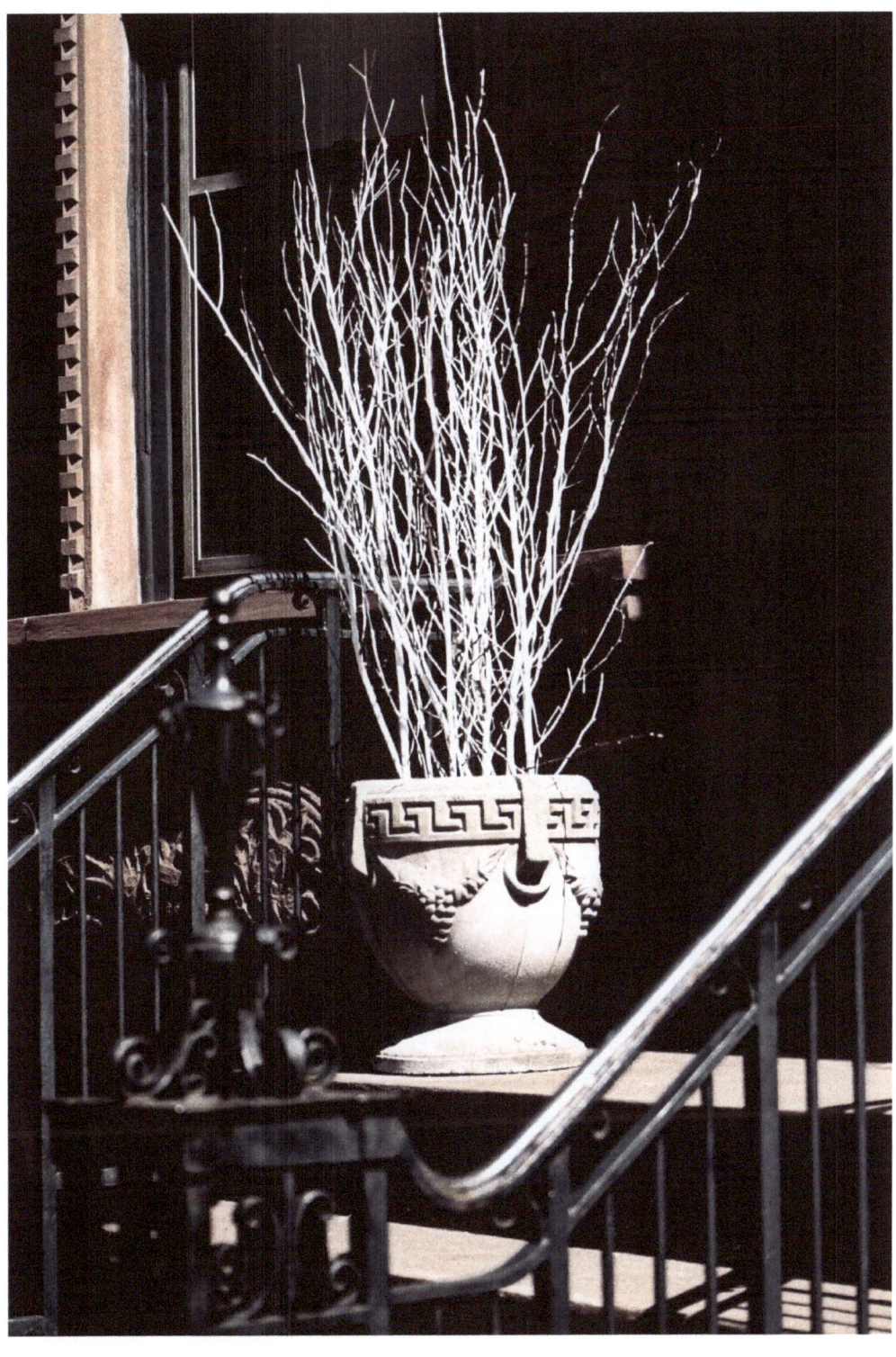

Albany Door

**State Street
Albany, NY**

On a beautiful Saturday morning in April, I took a walk through Albany and couldn't resist taking this striking doorway on State Street.

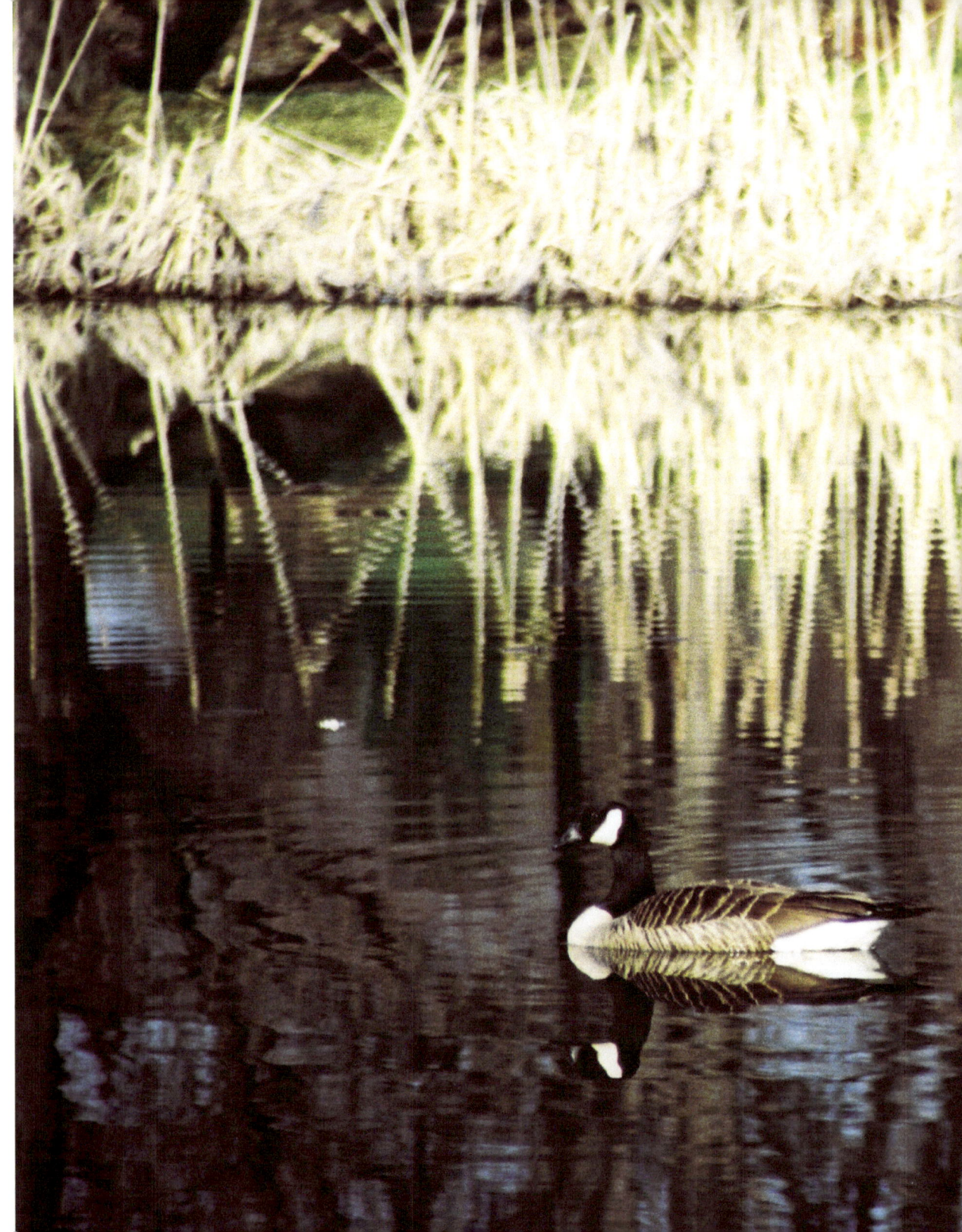

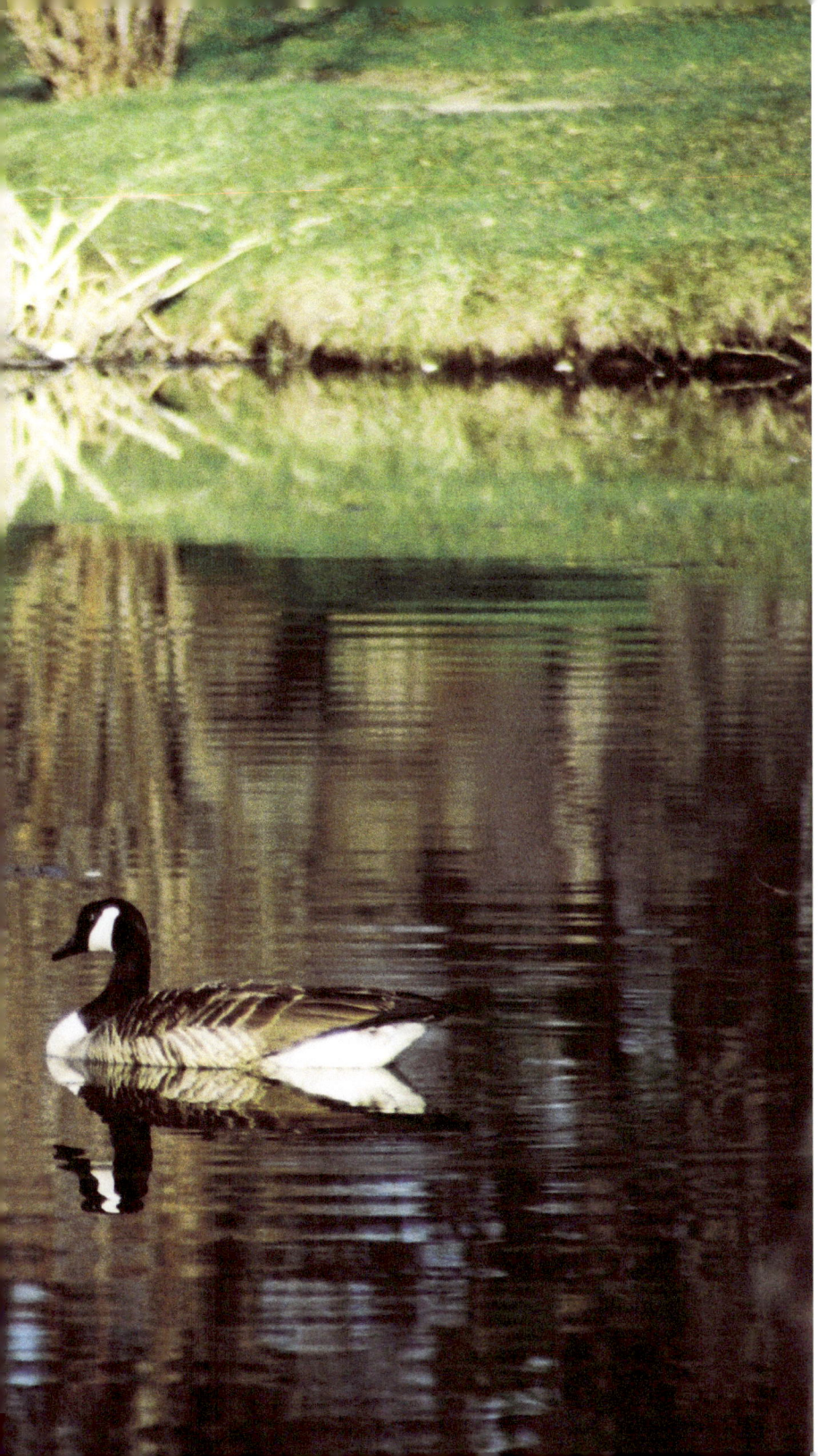

Canada Geese on a Quiet Day

Washington Park Albany, NY

Ahh, spring, when the first green comes to life in the park.

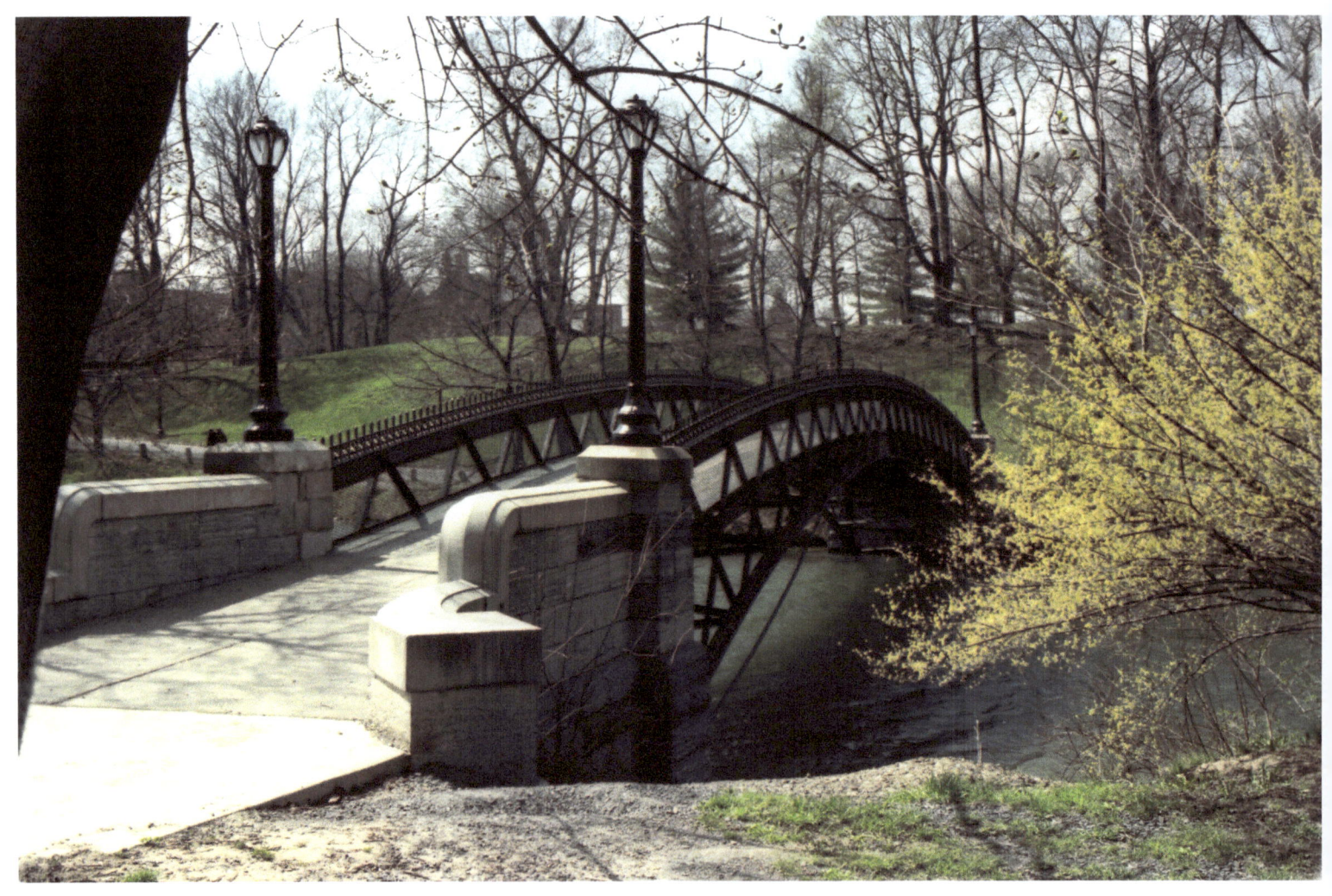

Footbridge, April
Washington Park, Albany, NY

This is a popular site for wedding and Easter pictures.

Lamp in the Snow

Washington Park Albany, NY

This shot reminds Jim of the lamp in the woods in *The Lion, The Witch, and the Wardrobe* by C.S. Lewis where it was "always winter but never Christmas."

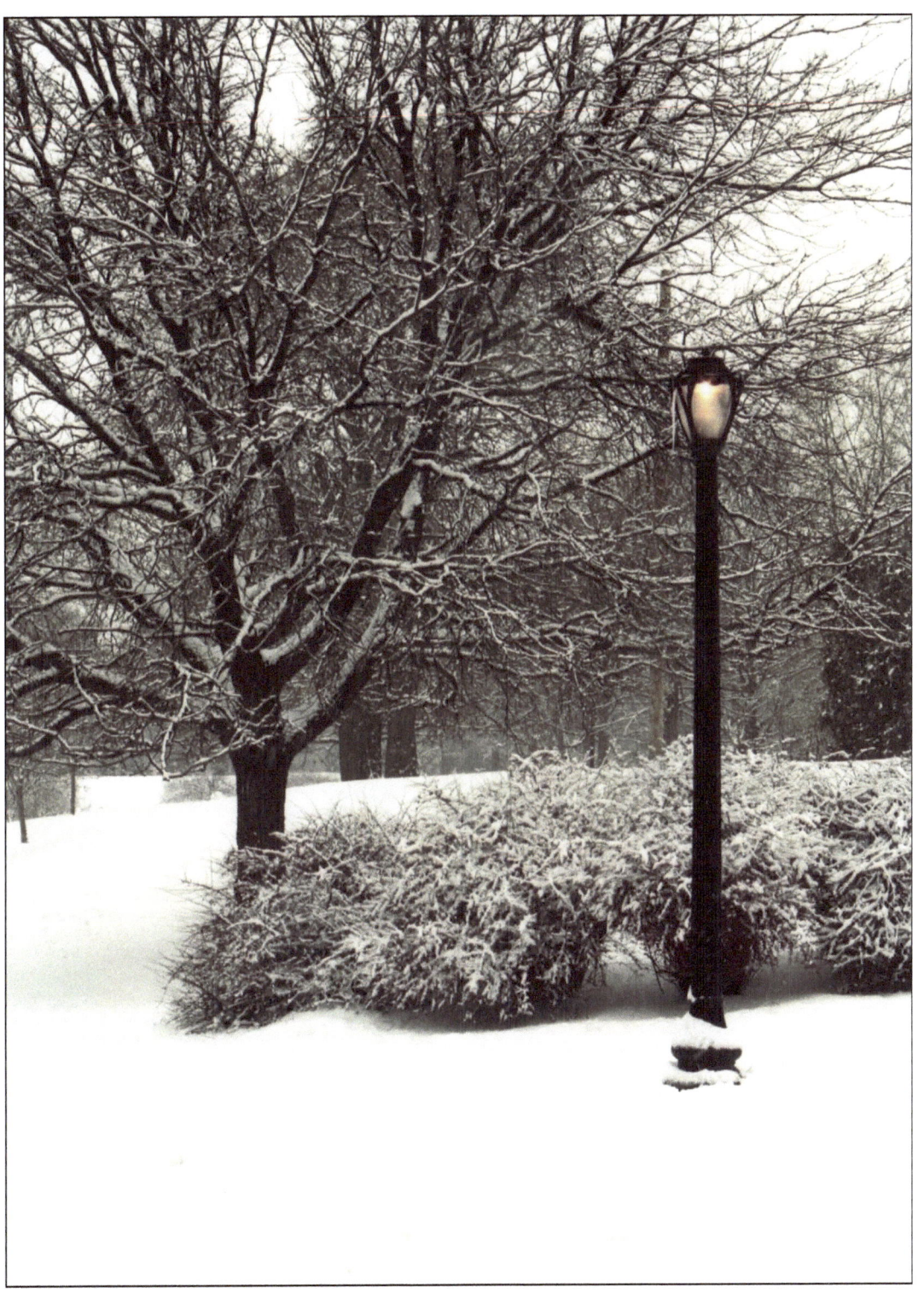

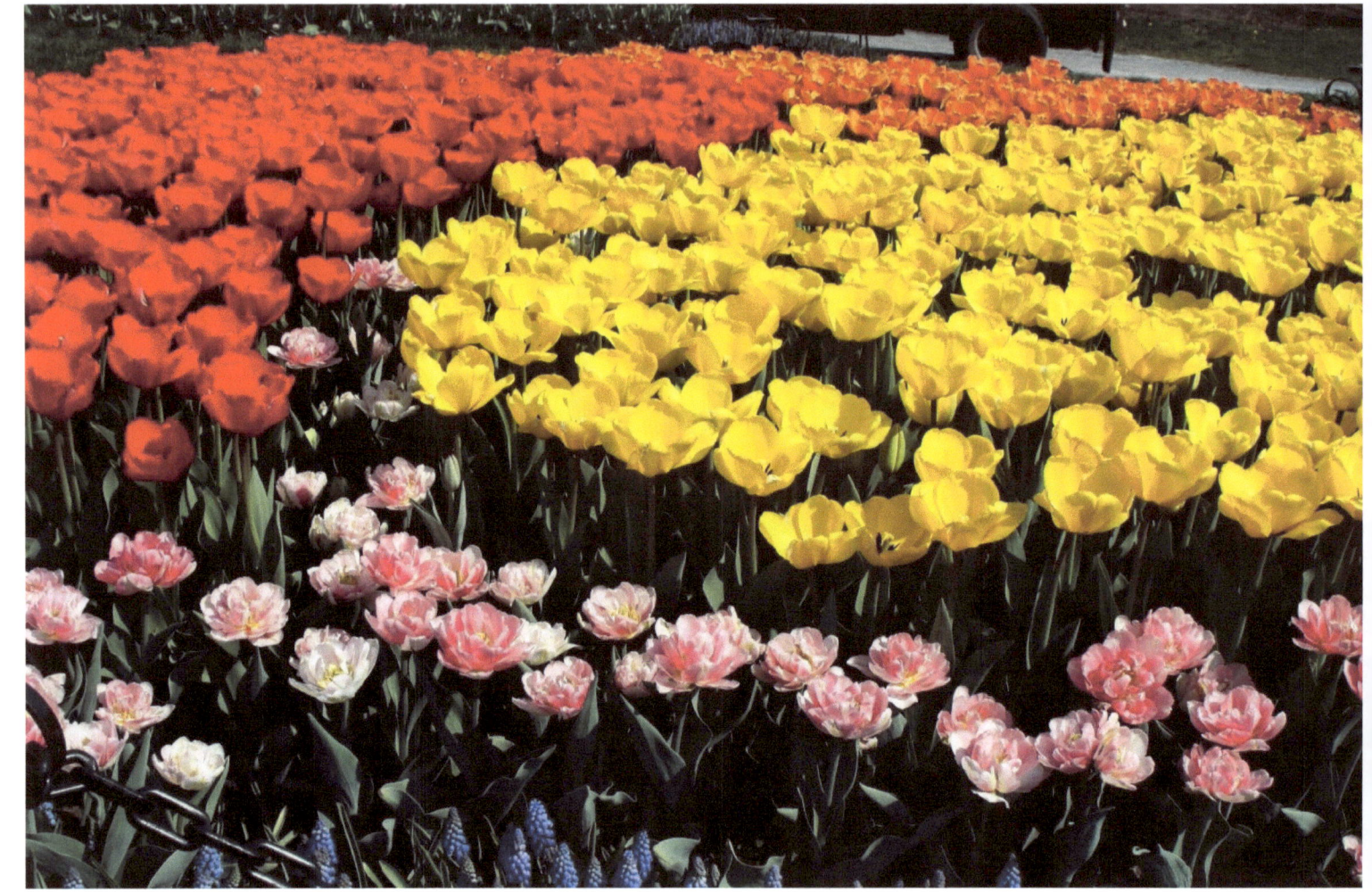

Albany Tulip Festival

Albany's official flower is the tulip, in recognition of Albany's Dutch founding in 1614. This historical connection is maintained in part through the Albany Tulip Festival, a highly anticipated spring tradition, when over 100,000 tulip blooms fill Washington Park with a sea of colors. Each year, in preparation for the festival, State Street is scrubbed, keeping alive the Dutch tradition of scrubbing the streets before a large celebration.

Washington Park hosts thousands who come to see the tulips, witness the coronation of the Tulip

Anne and I had a front row seat to the activities.

As a historical note, Albany supplied Holland with tulip bulbs to help replace the ones eaten by the population in the last winter of World War II.

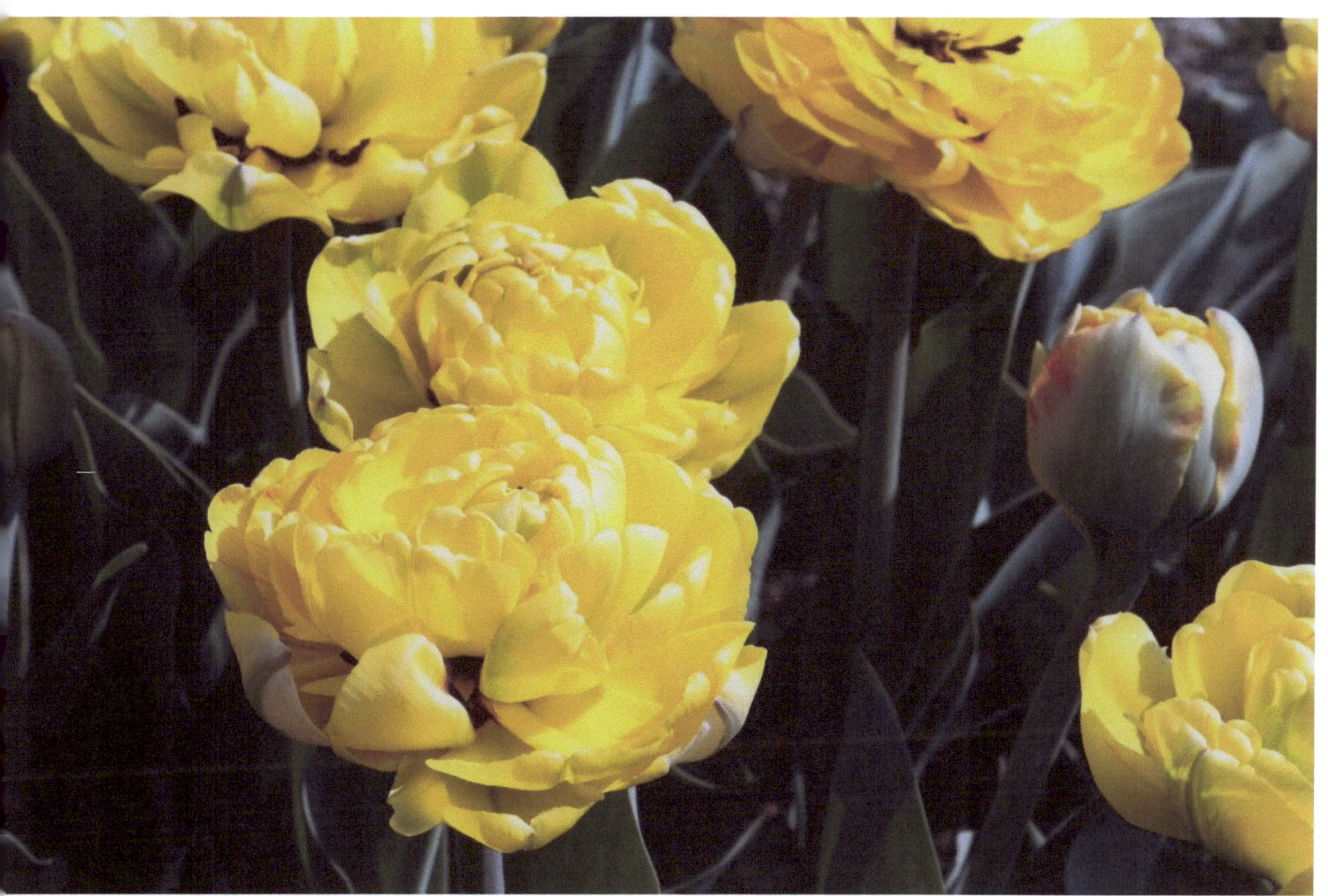

Cherry Blossom Cascade

Washington Park
Albany, NY

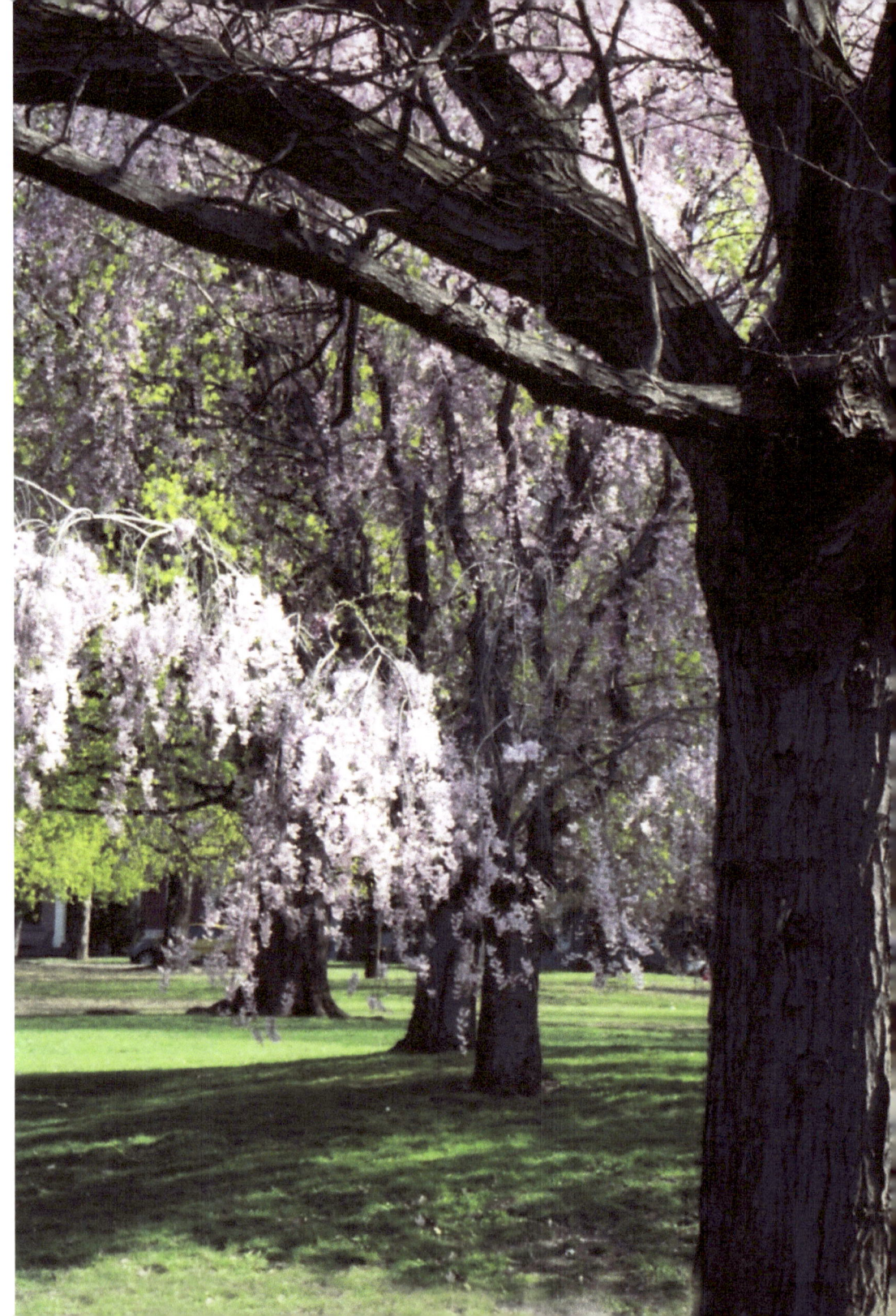

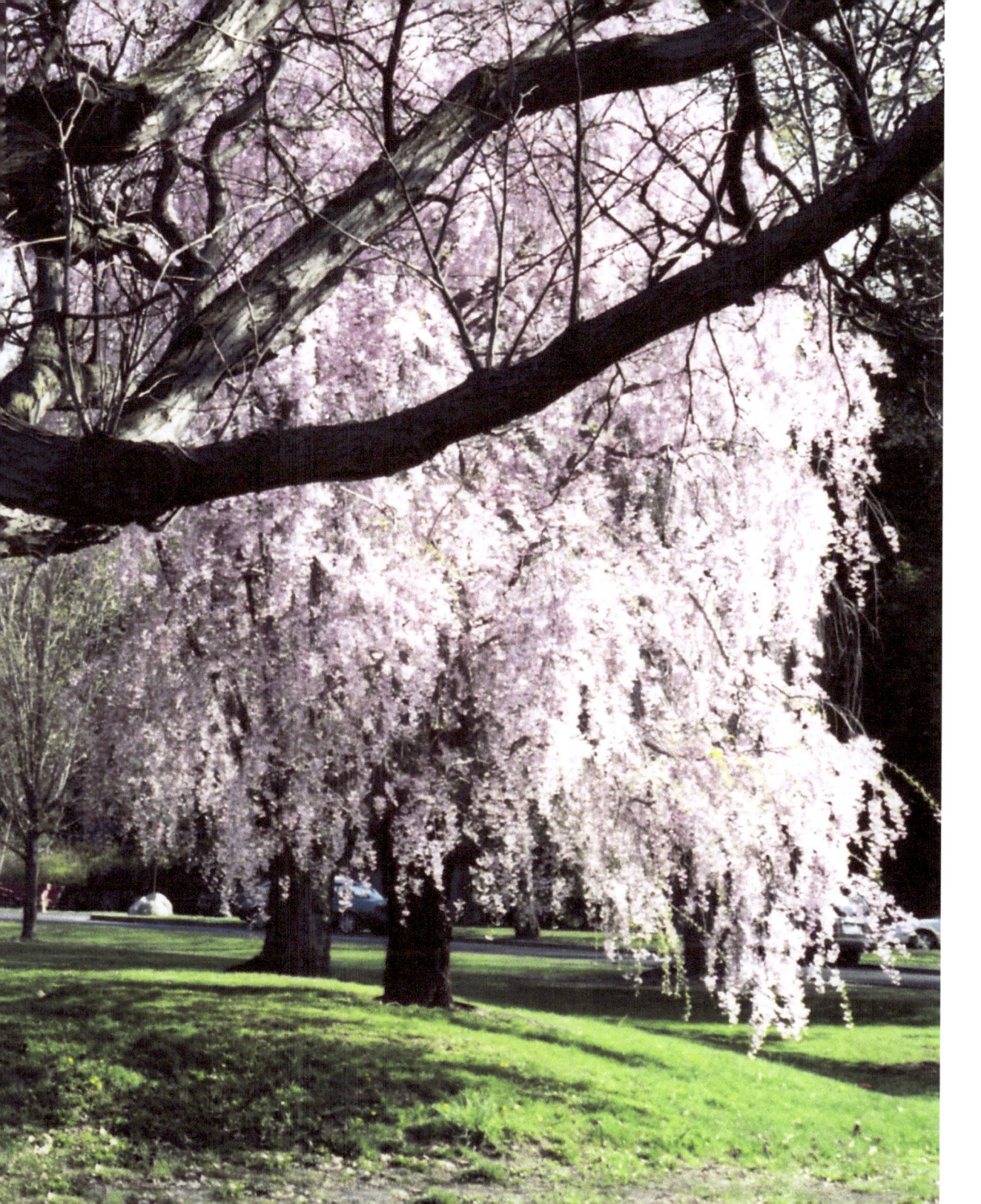

The Adirondacks

Our love affair with the Adirondacks began in 1954 when Anne's parents, Sara and Howard Cammack, purchased a camp in a summer community one mile south of Essex, NY, on the western shore of Lake Champlain, with a stunning view of the lake, the Green Mountains, and the Vermont shore.

Over the next 60 years our family enjoyed summers on Lake Champlain taking advantage of the opportunities to sail, swim, and hike. Summer life revolved around our camp and friends in the Crater Club and the community in the Town of Essex.

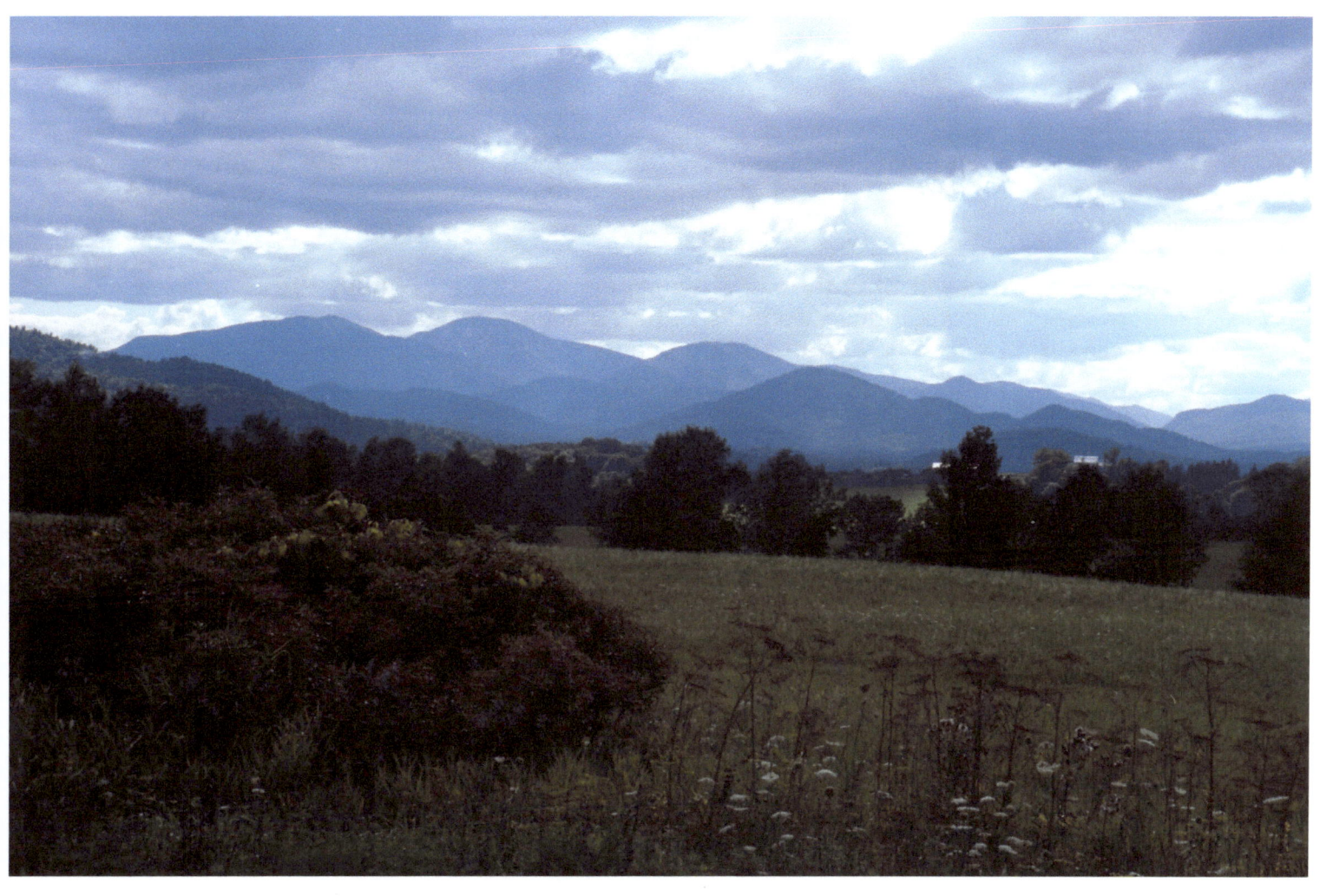

Adirondack Mountains
Looking West to the High Peaks

One of our favorite views of the High Peaks. Rocky Peak and Giant Mountain are the two peaks on the left.

The Crater Club

The Crater Club was our summer community for 60 years. Our first Crater Club camp, called Corners, was purchased by Anne's parents and had a stunning view of the Vermont shore and the Green Mountains. Anne's brother, David, and his family used Corners in July and we stayed there in August.

In 1972, we purchased Stand Easy, our own camp, with an equally stunning view of Vermont. In 1992, we added Captain's Cabin, a separate sleeping cabin for Anne and myself, so our children and grandchildren could enjoy the main house.

The Crater Club is a 600 acre seasonal residential community on the shore of Lake Champlain founded and developed in the early 1900s by naturalist John Bird Burnham. Currently, the Crater Club consists of over 40 homes, a clubhouse, playing fields, clay tennis courts, and a waterfront featuring a permanent pier and a screened building known as Burnham's Landing.

Our family enjoyed swimming, sailing, hiking, tennis, reading, and watching the view. We especially enjoyed sailing and were active members of the Split Rock Yacht Club, participating in their weekly Cape Cod Knockabout sailboat races whenever we were at the Crater Club. Over the years our family owned and sailed a Sailfish, several Sunfish, a Hobie Cat, a Champlain Knockabout (Nancy Anne), two Cape Cod Knockabouts (Valcour, Plastic Wood) and a Tanzer 22 (Arcturus).

We held our family reunions at the Crater Club.

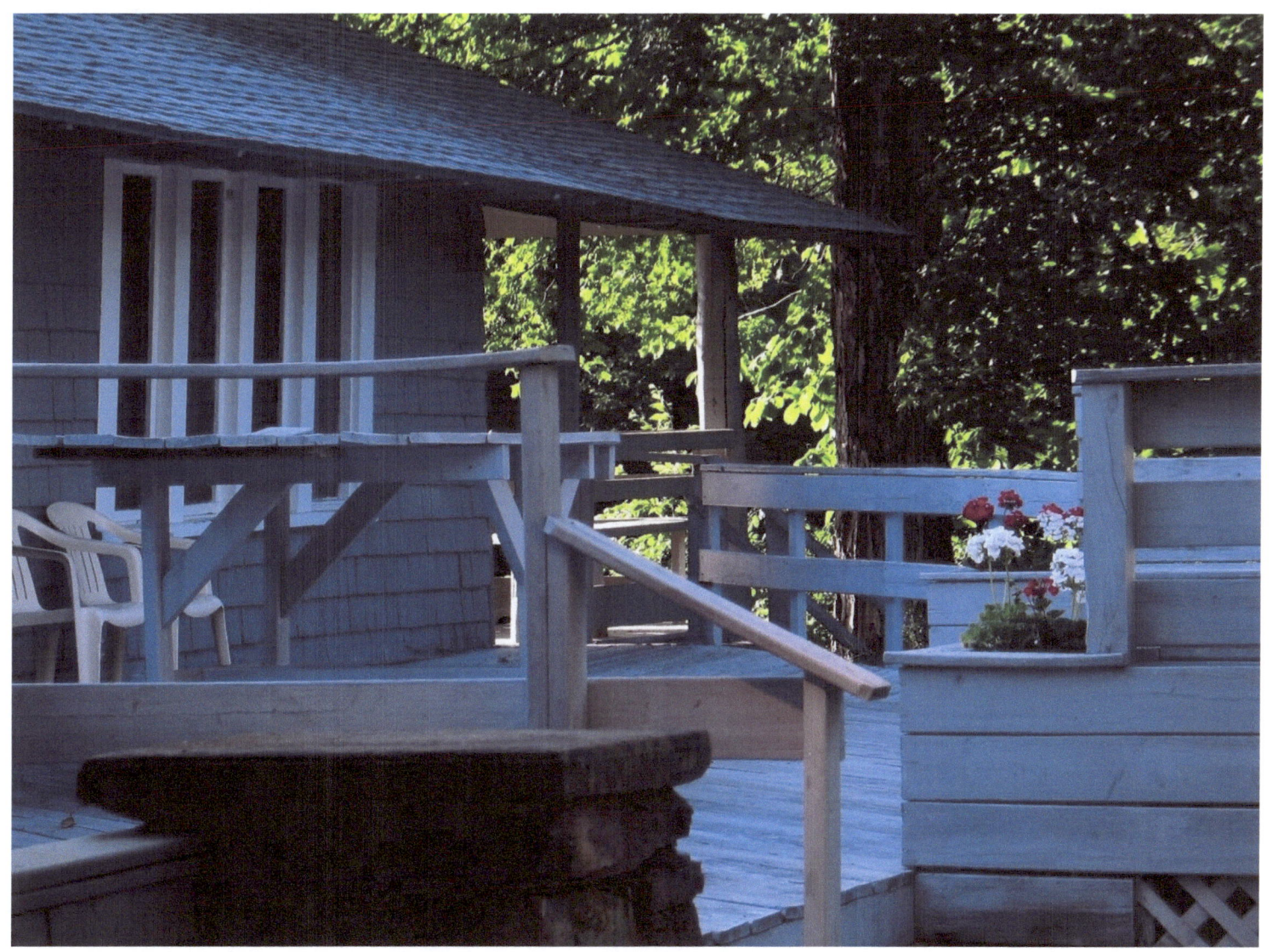

Crater Club Clubhouse Side Porch

Photo by Luke Brewster

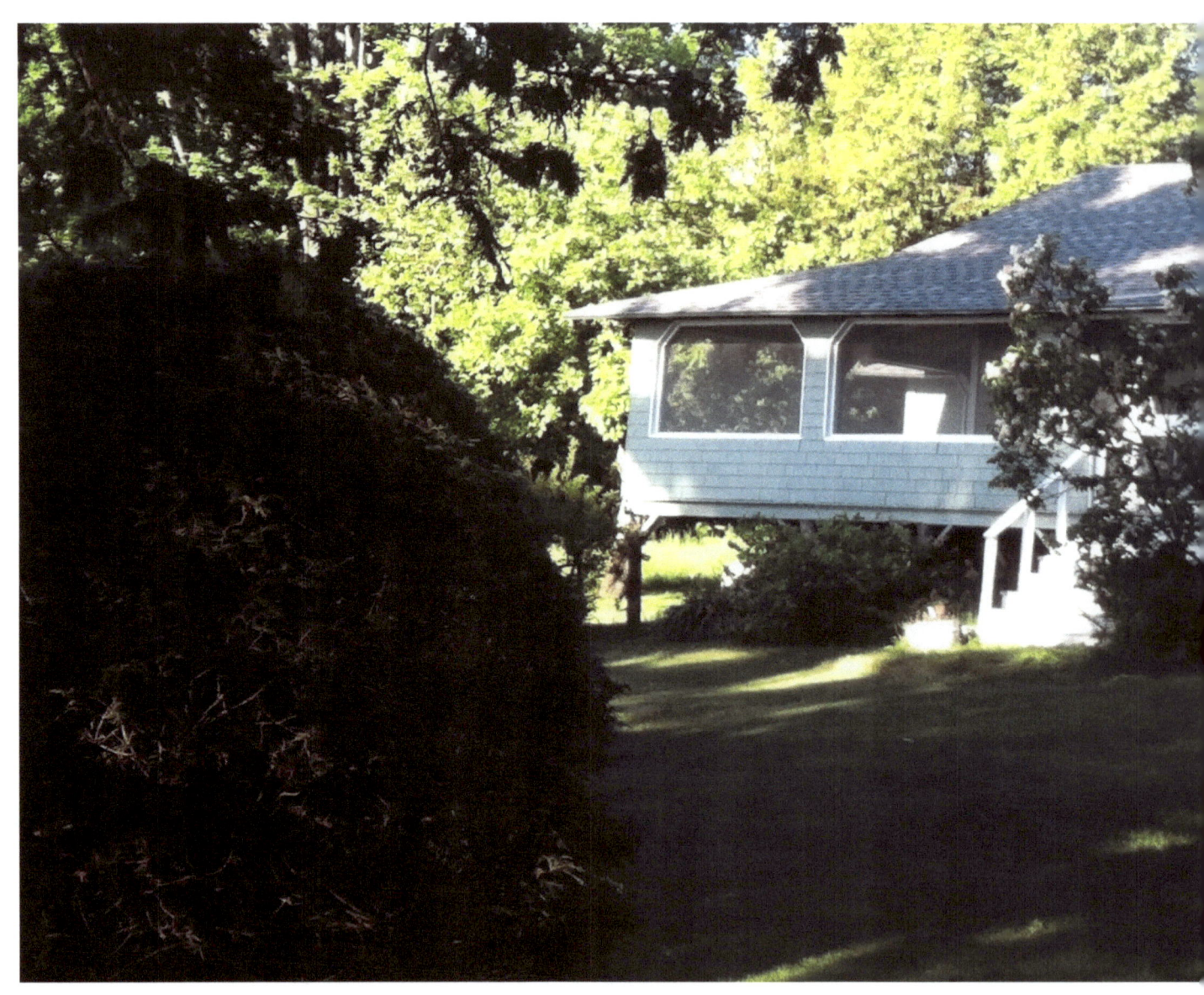

Stand Easy - Our Camp at the Crater Club

Our summer retreat from 1972 - 2014

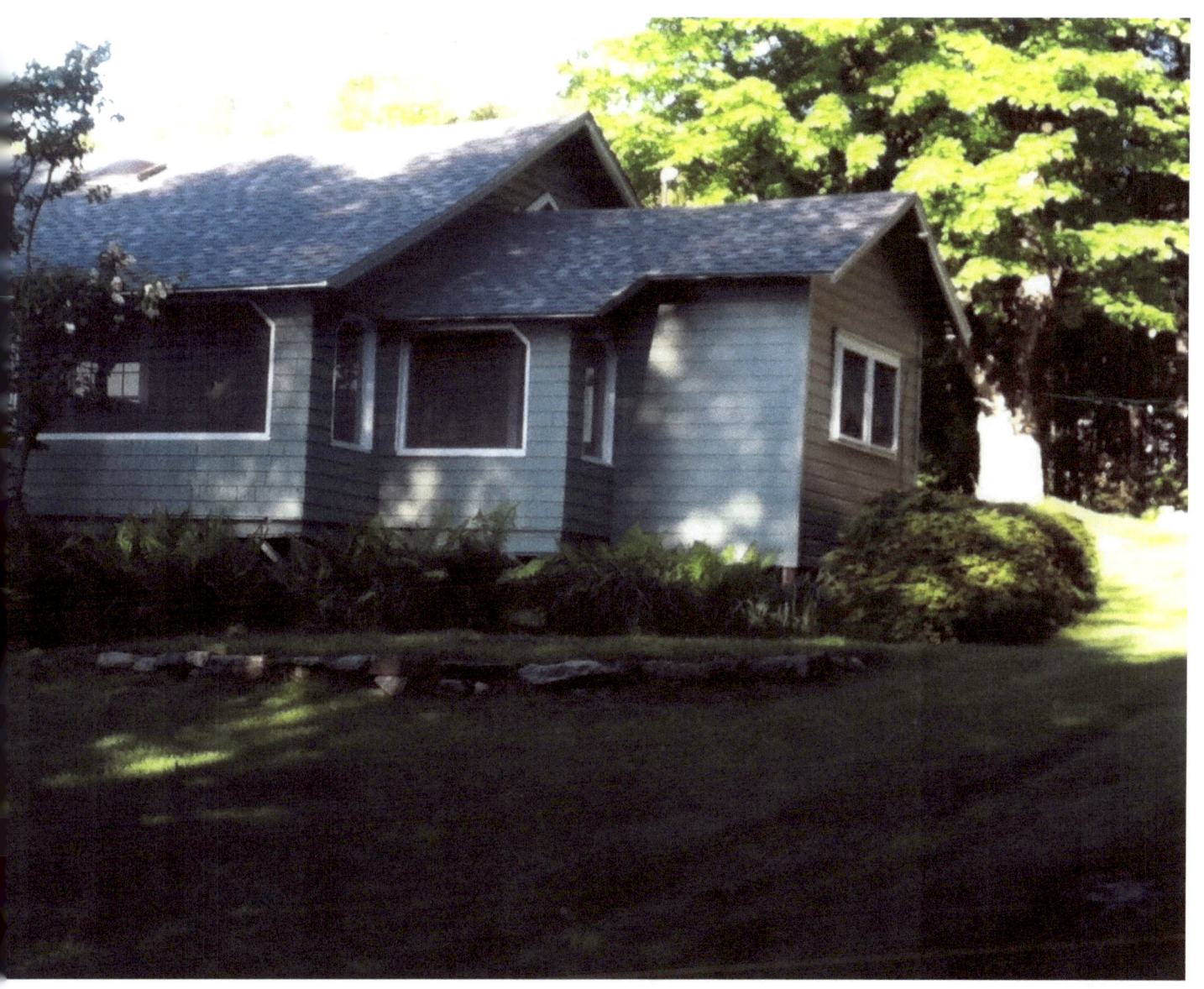

Photo by James Burd Brewster

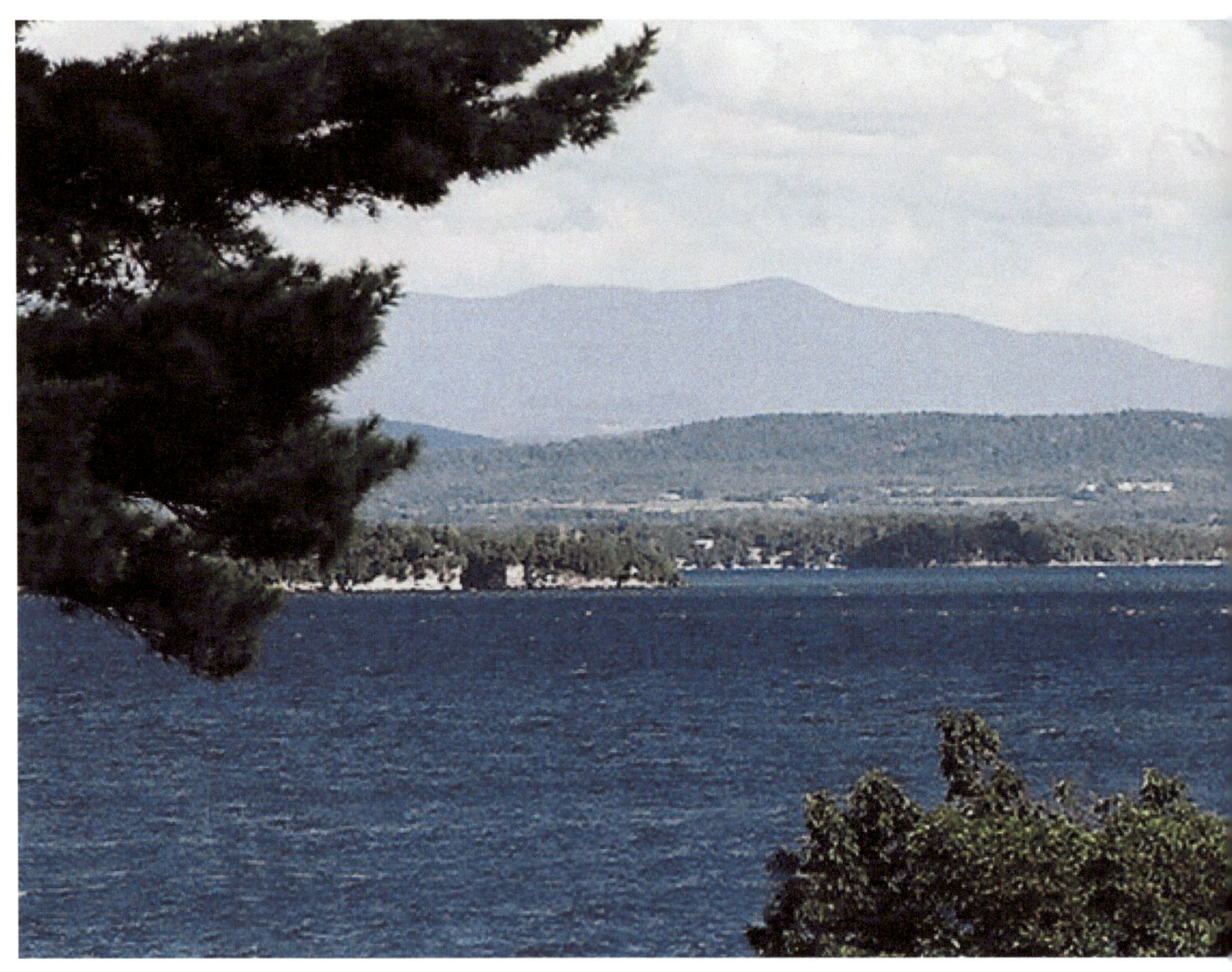

Split Rock from Captain's Cabin

Called Roche Regio by the Indians, Split Rock was the boundary between the Mohawks and Algonquin's.

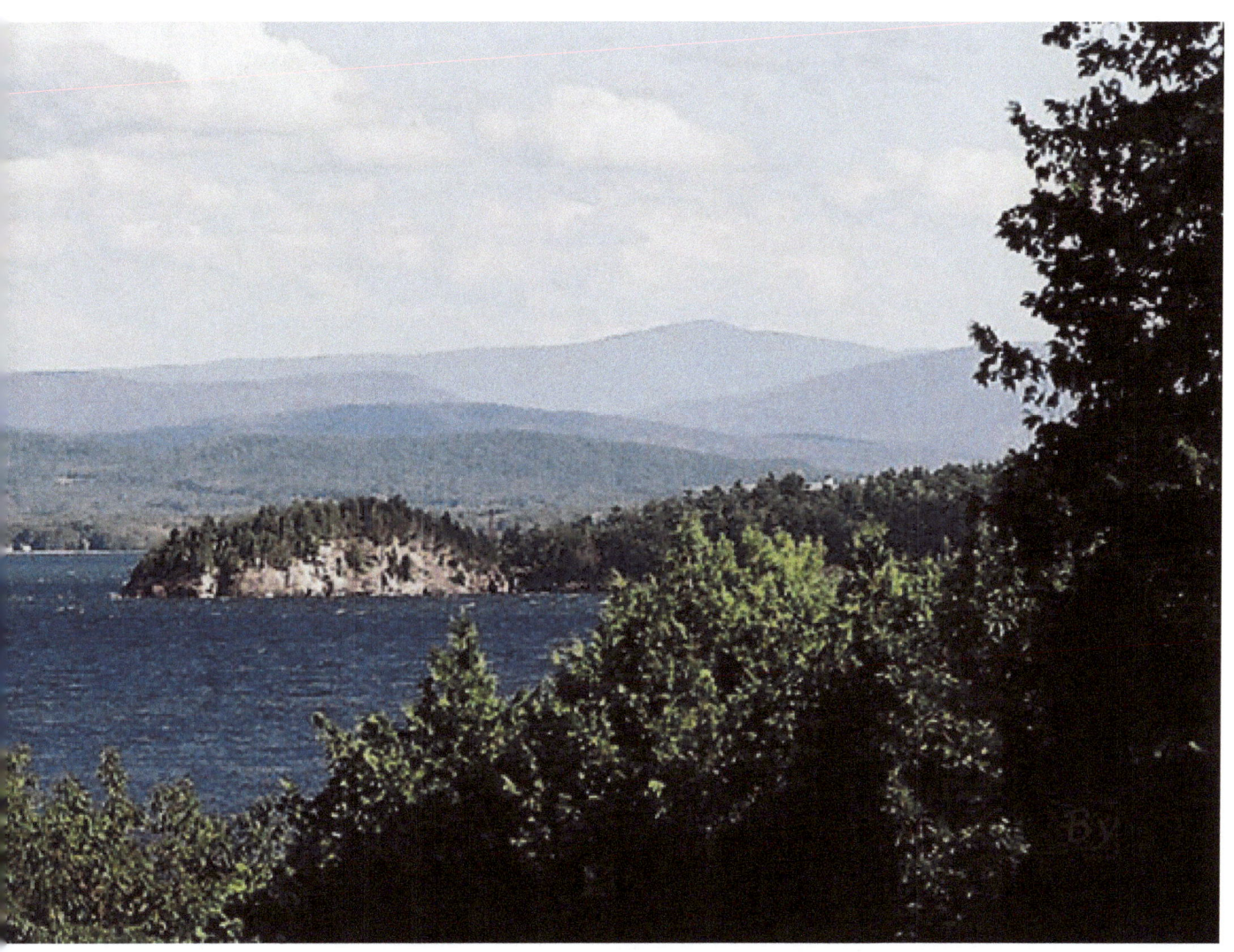

This is one of many photos I took over the past twenty plus years from the porch of Captain's Cabin, each in different light, weather, and wind. During the time that has elapsed since we built Captain's Cabin, this view has gotten smaller and in a few more years it will be obscured by foliage growth.

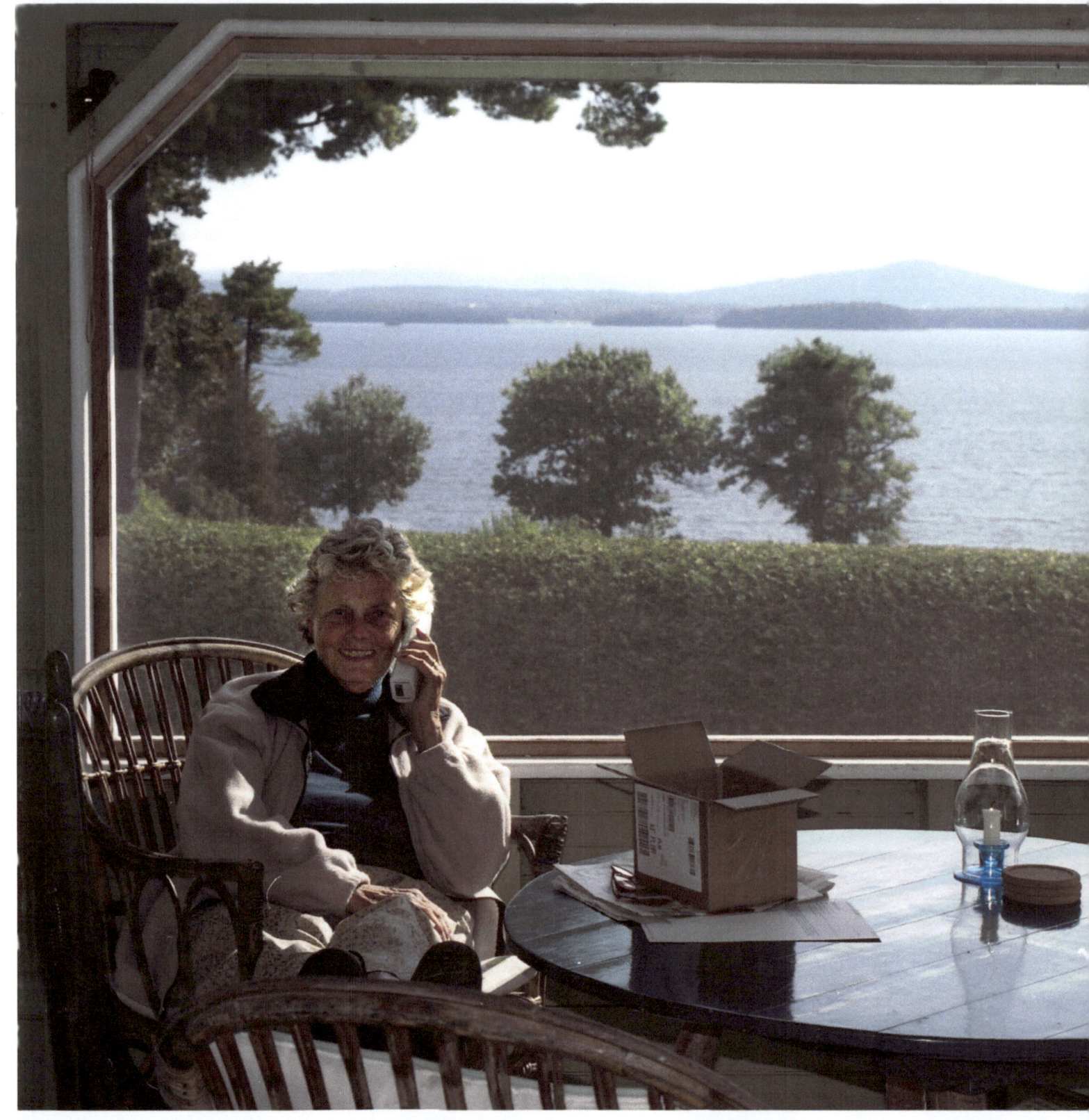

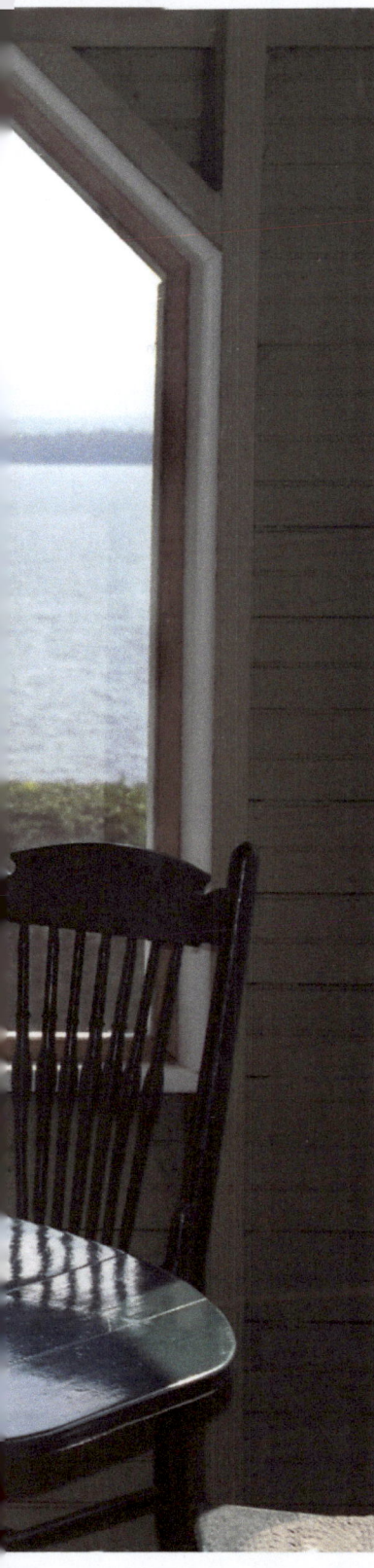

After the Mail

This is quite typical of Anne on the porch of Stand Easy. I just happened to have my camera at my side on this beautiful day and snapped the picture.

I had to work a bit in Photoshop to balance exposure between the foreground and background.

Mount Philo can be seen on the Vermont shore.

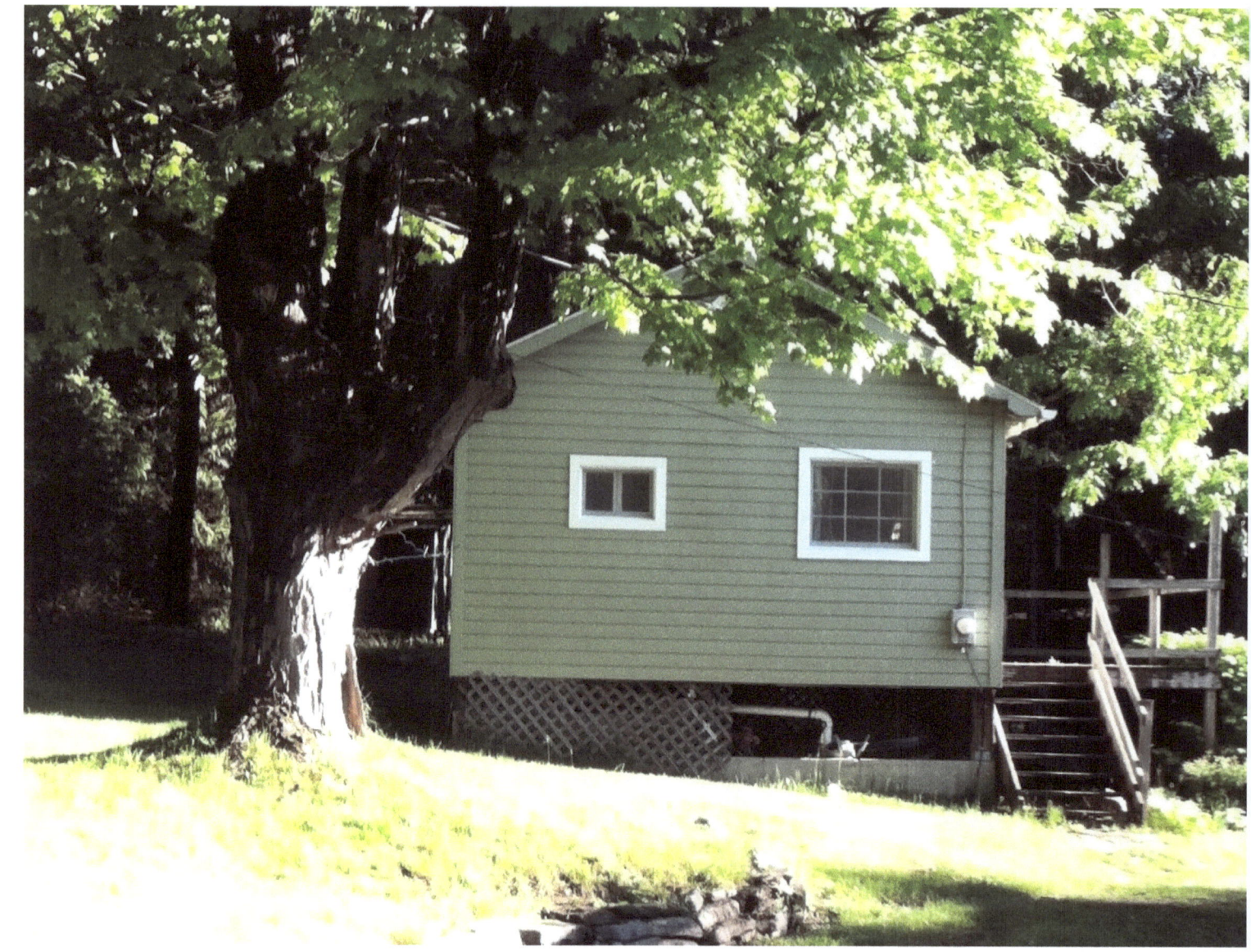

Captain's Cabin

This is our sleeping cabin, built in the summer of 1992 by our children and grandchildren. From the porch, Anne and I had a wonderful view of Lake Champlain and Split Rock and spent many evenings enjoying the ever-changing, always-interesting display of wind, waves, and clouds.

Photo by James Burd Brewster

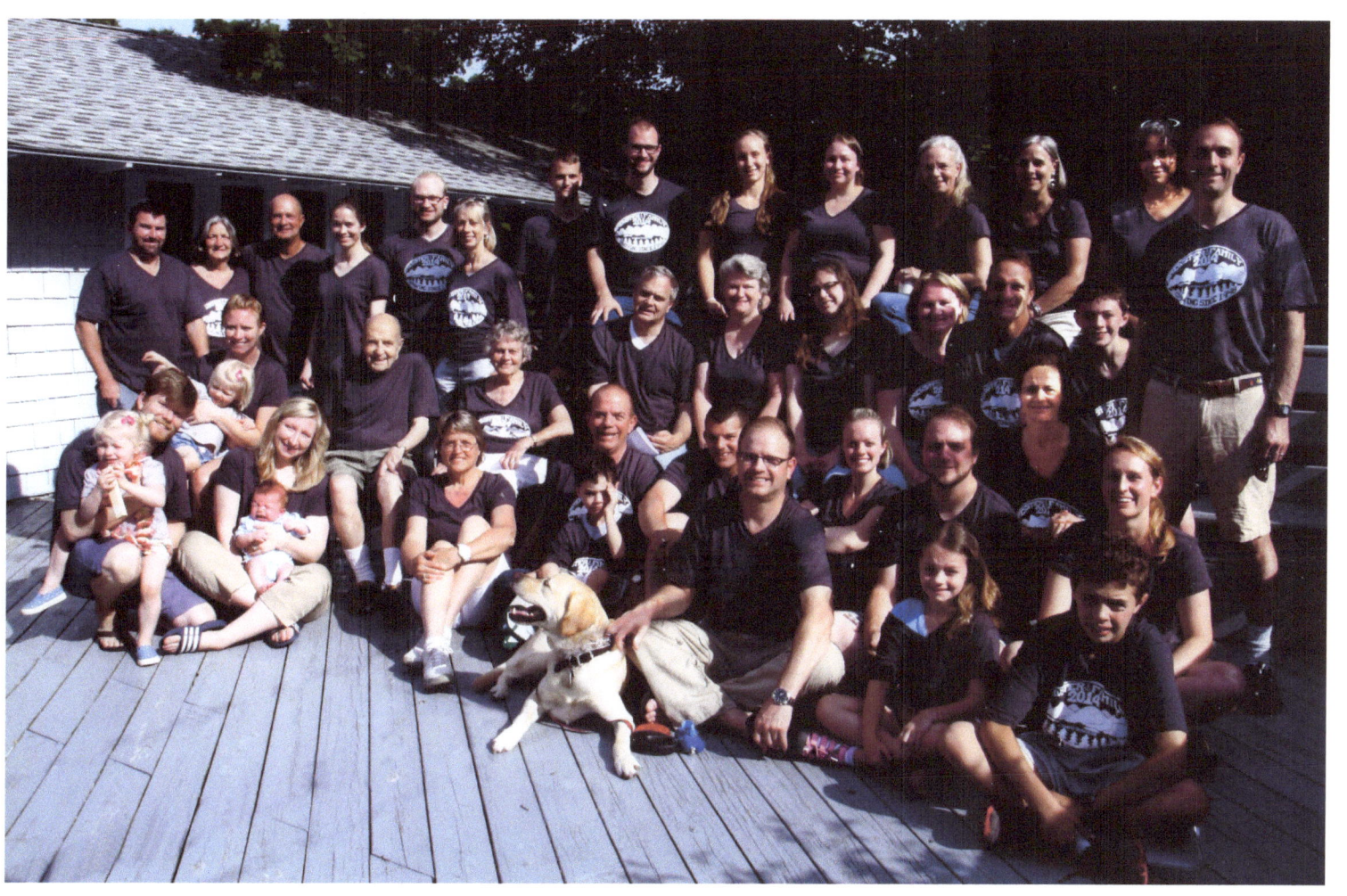

Brewster Family Reunion - 2014
Crater Club, Essex, NY

Ben and Anne results: Seven children, nineteen grandchildren, and twenty-one great-grandchildren and counting.

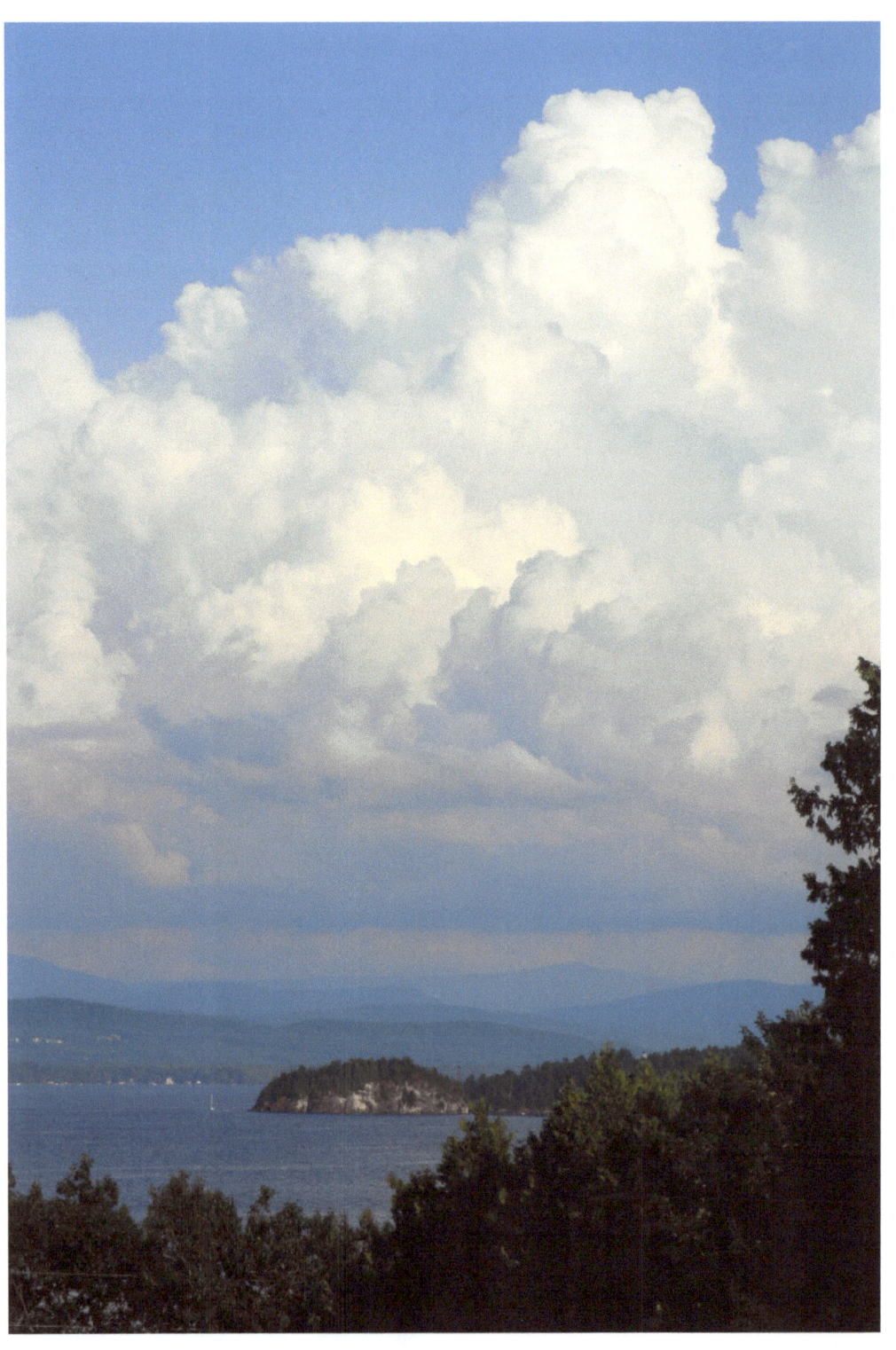

Champlain Clouds

Clouds over Lake Champlain were always fascinating to watch, yet on some days their size, shape, color, and beauty became transfixing.

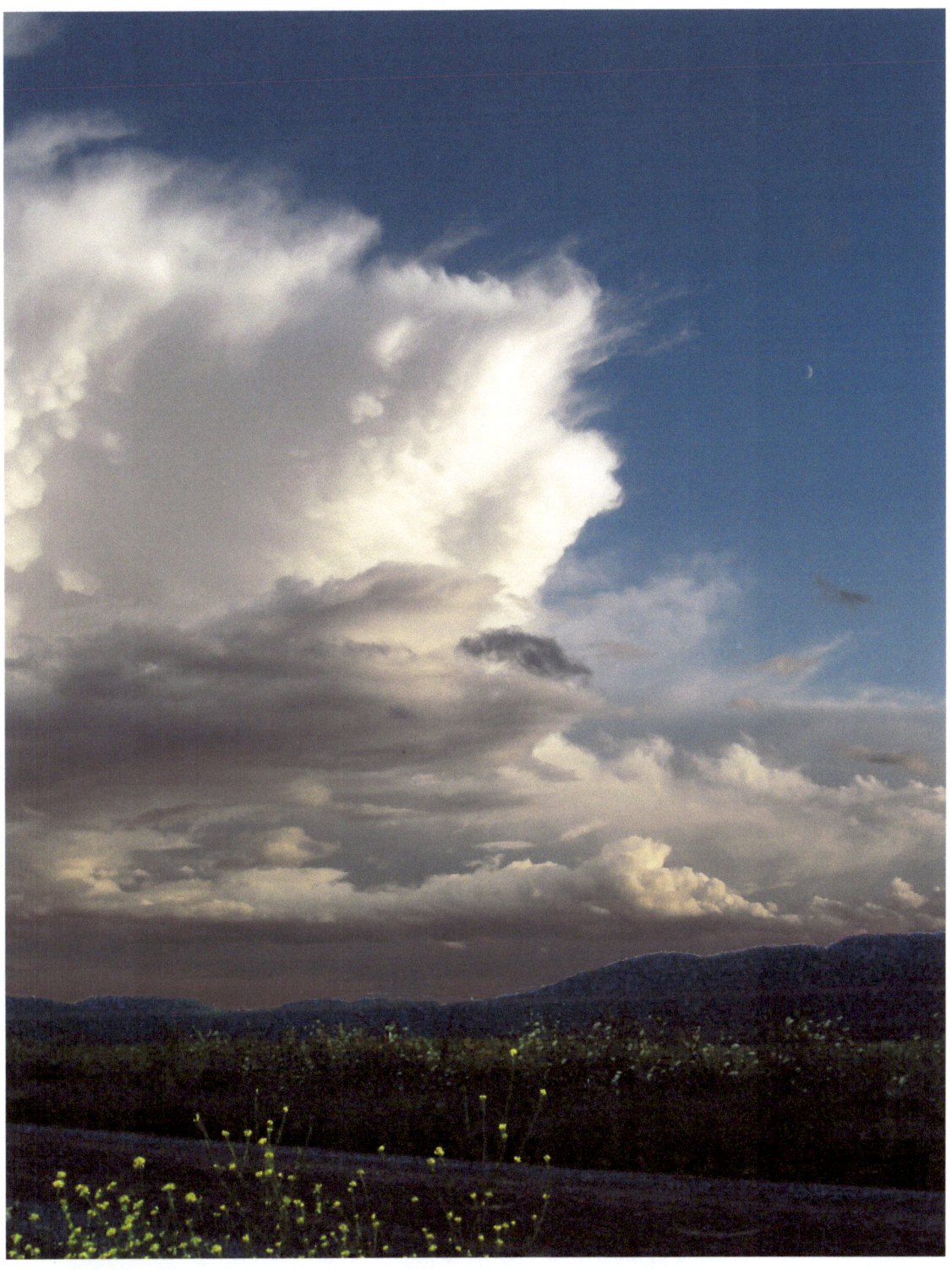

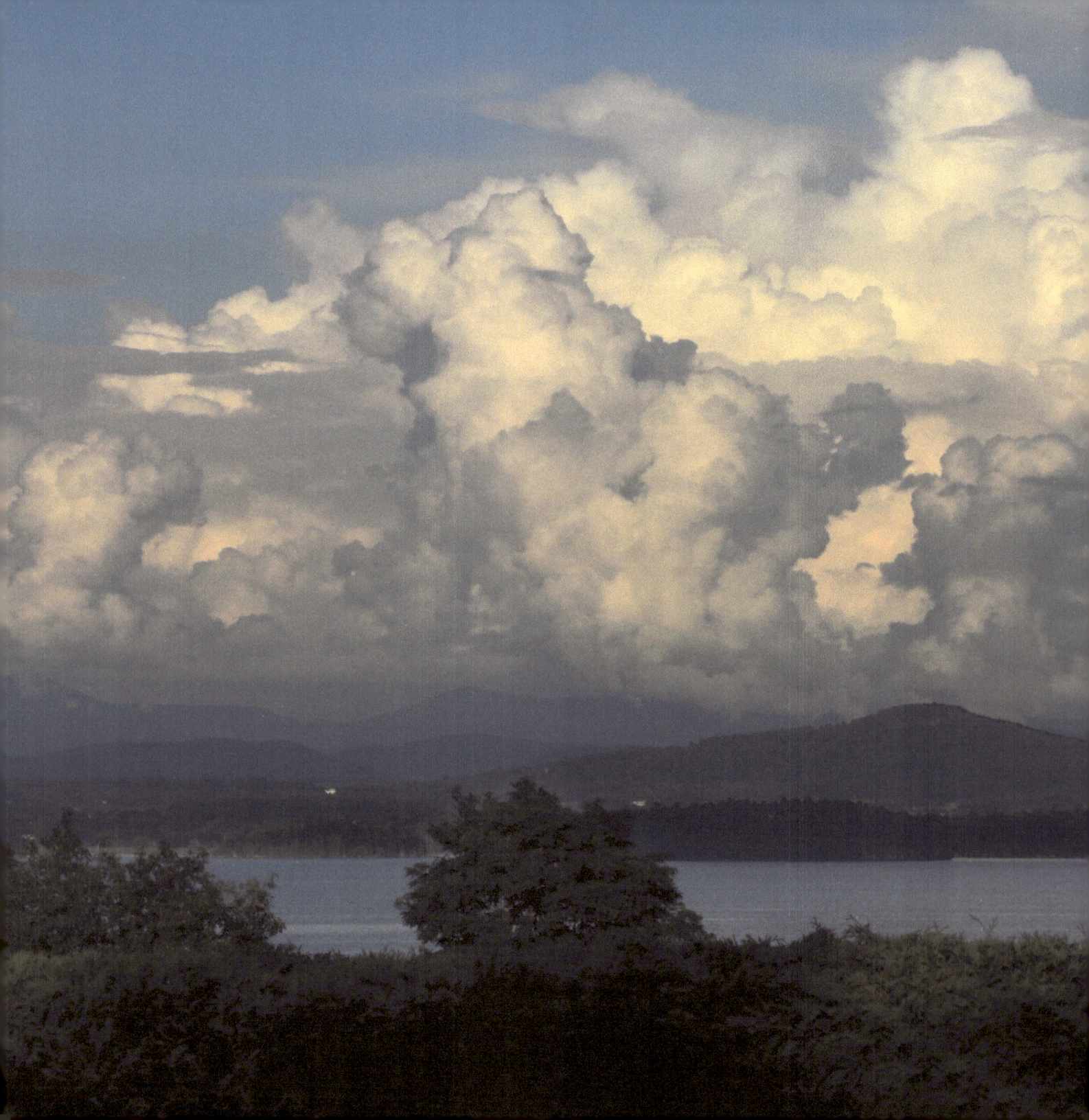

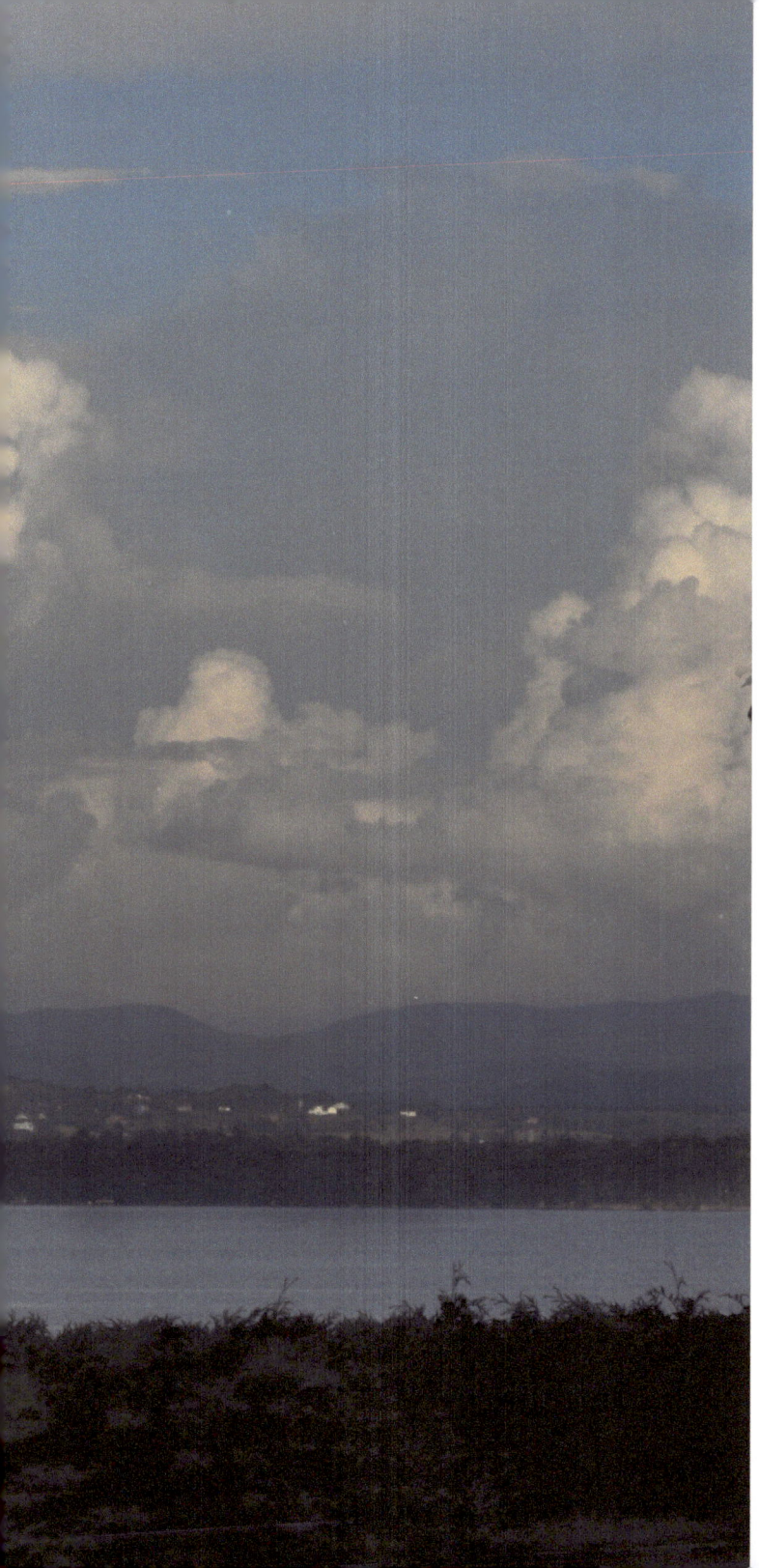

Clouds Over Mt. Philo

Another spectacular evening display following the afternoon's thunder shower.

Taken from the porch of Stand Easy.

Next page

Supper Table View

This was our breakfast, lunch, and supper view as we sat and ate at the table on the front porch of Stand Easy.

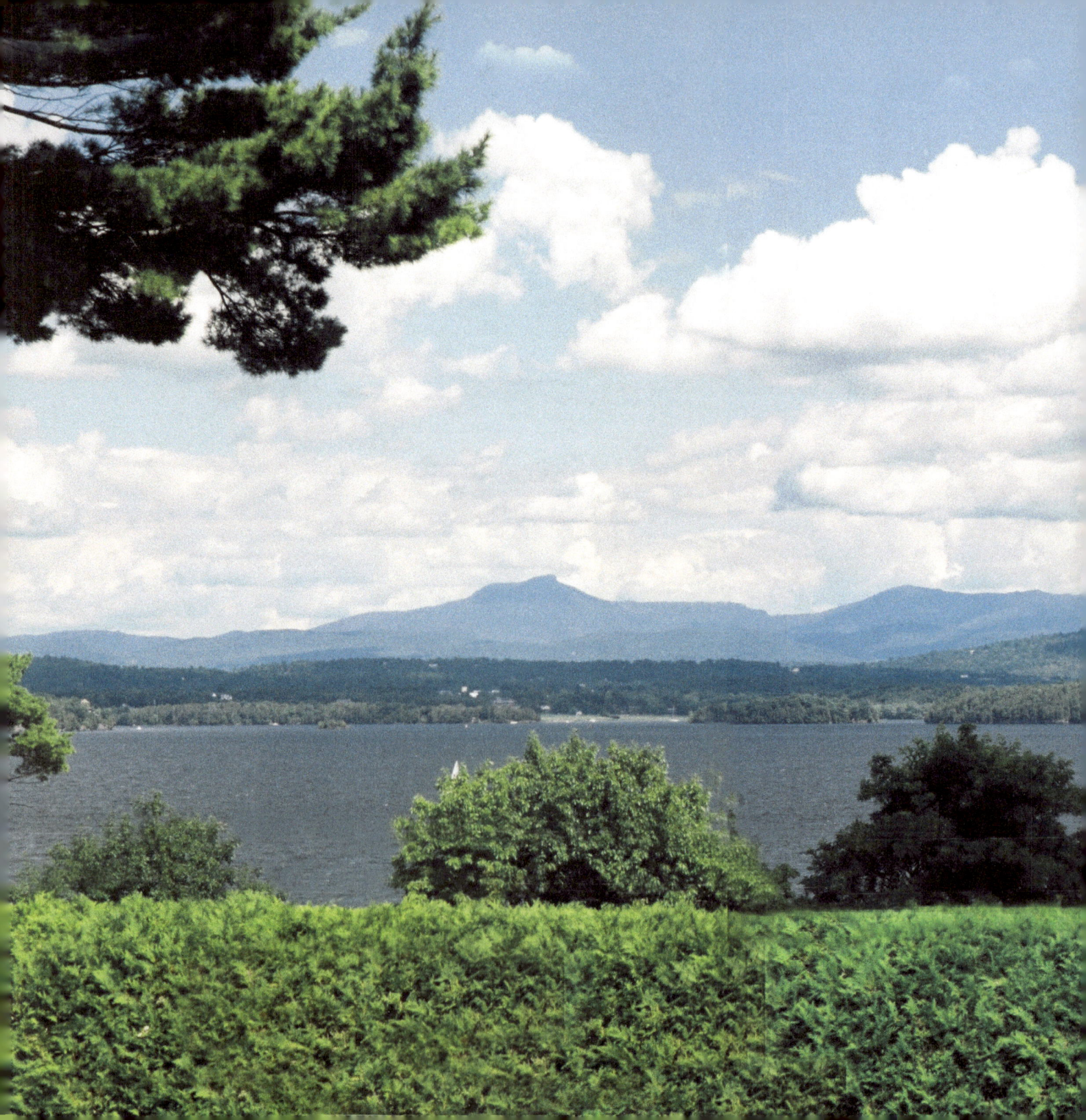

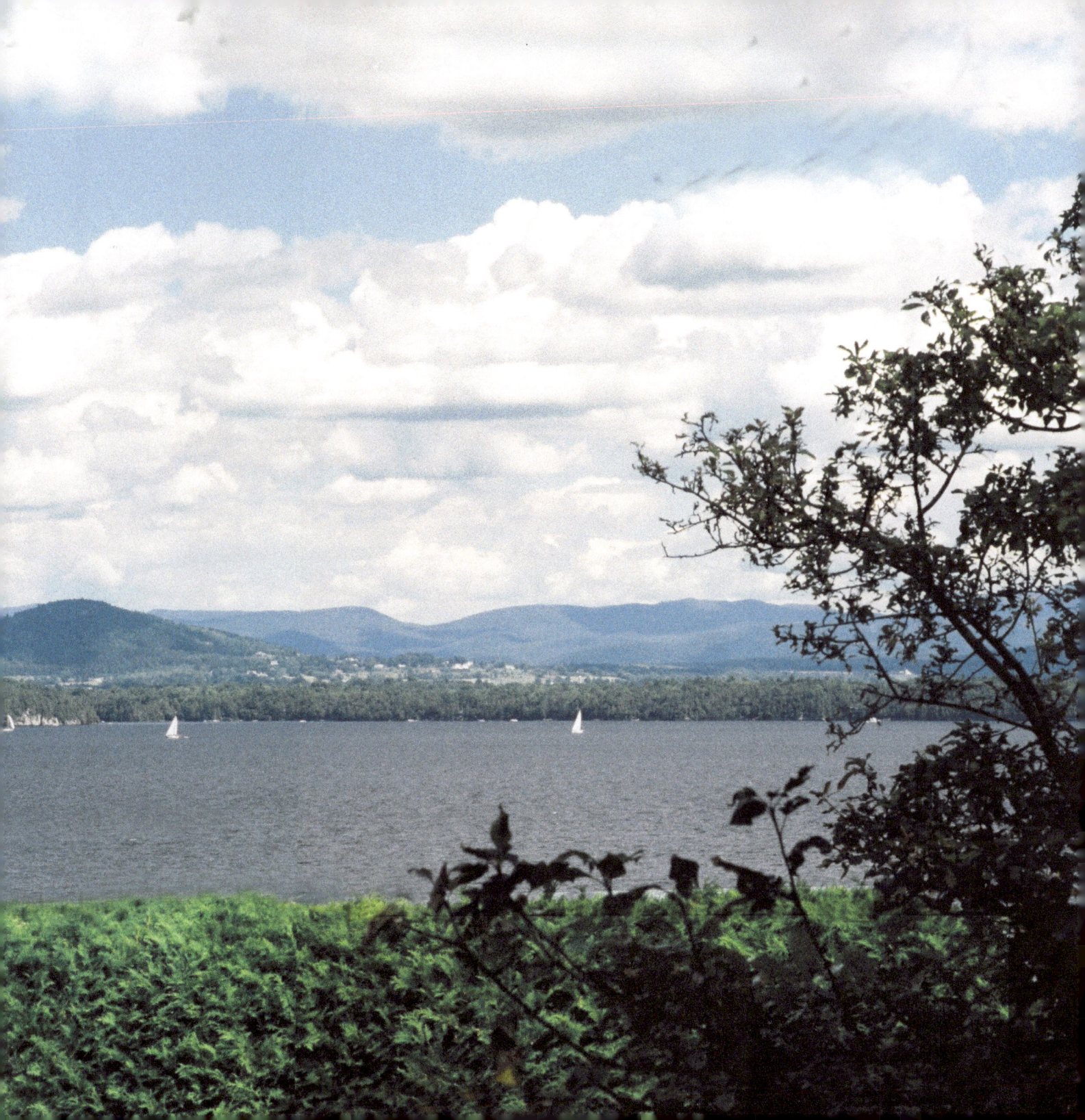

Town of Essex, NY

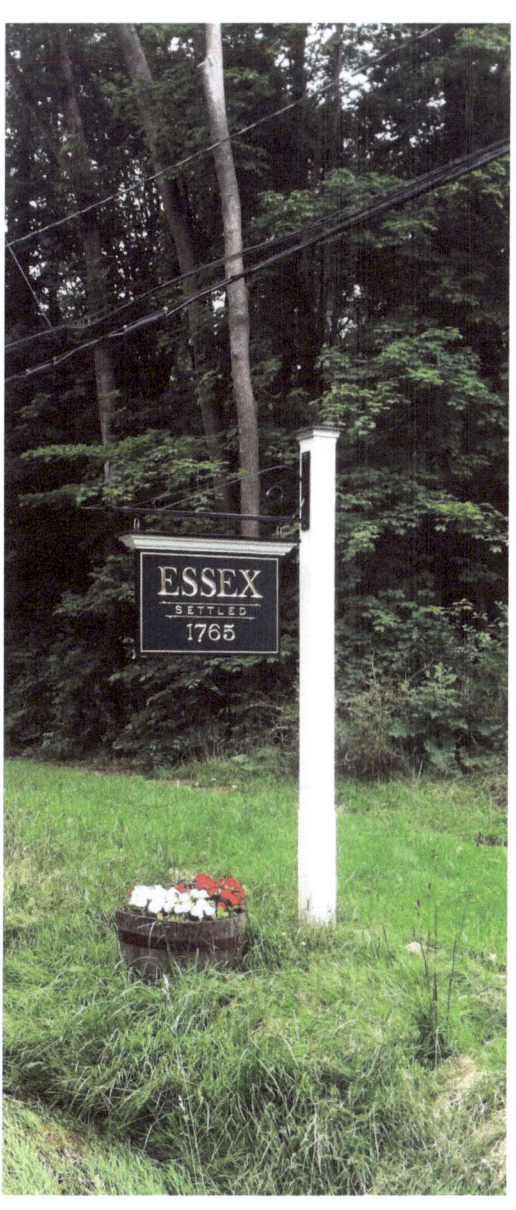

The Town of Essex is one mile north of the Crater Club and is home to the Fire Department, the Essex Marina, St. John's Episcopal church, a library, several craft stores, and the Adirondack Art Gallery. Essex is also the New York terminus of the Champlain Ferry to Charlotte, VT. In the 50's and 60's, we did our shopping at Tart's store in Essex.

Essex was part of a land grant made to Louis Joseph Robart by French King Louis XV. Robert lost the grant when the British took over the region after 1763. In 1765, landowner and investor, William Gilliland, founded Willsboro with the intention of creating a baronial estate like those of the lower Hudson River. Essex was formed in 1805 from a part of the Town of Willsboro and became an important Lake Champlain port and shipbuilding location, remaining so until the arrival of railroads in the region in 1849.

The presence of the ferry terminal in Essex helps maintain the life of the community which now consists of quaint shops, cafes, and restaurants. Essex is unique in its placement on the National Register of Historic Places as the entire town, including the Essex Village Historic District, the Essex County Home and Farm, and the Foothills Baptist Church, is listed in the Registry.

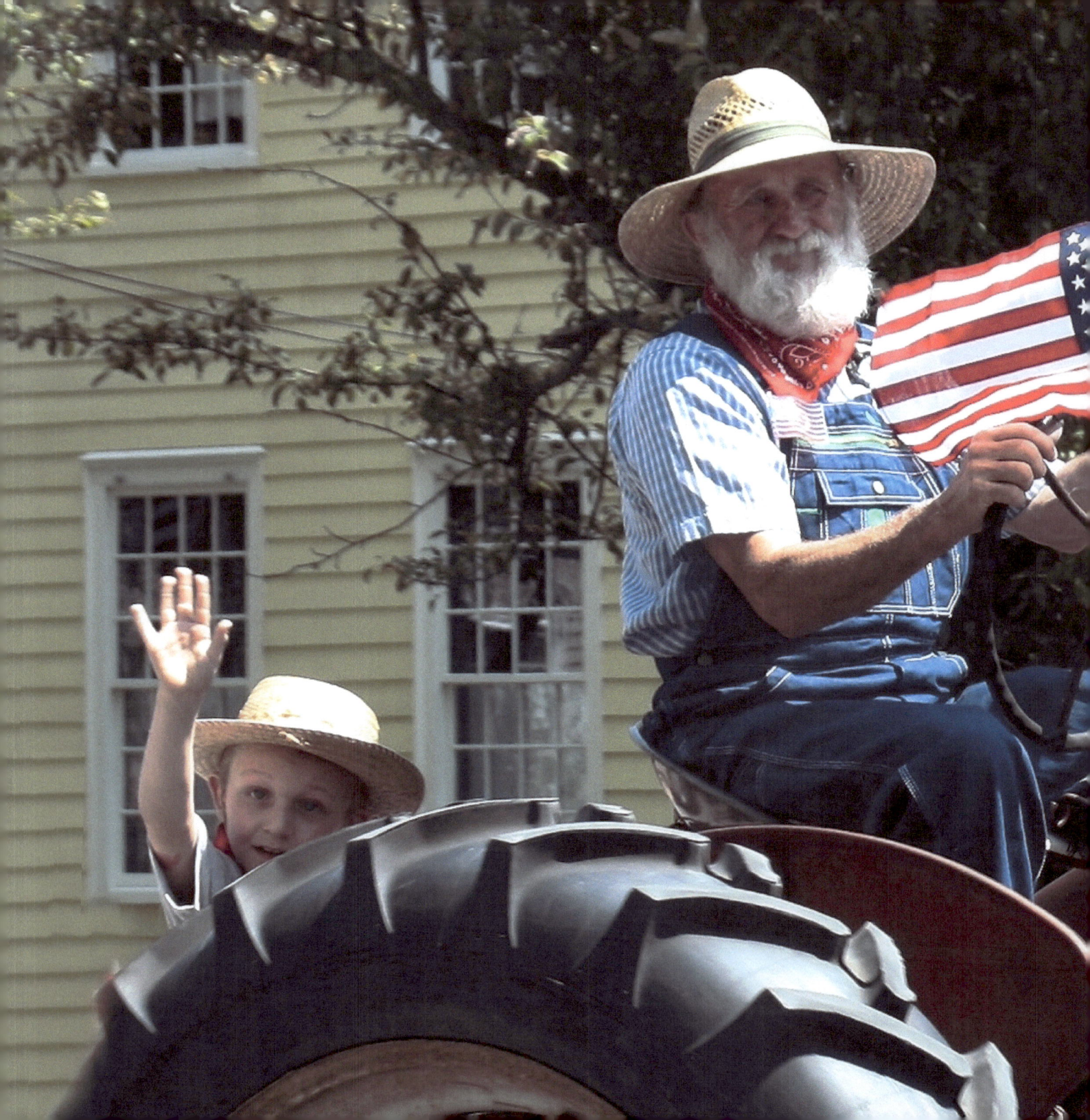

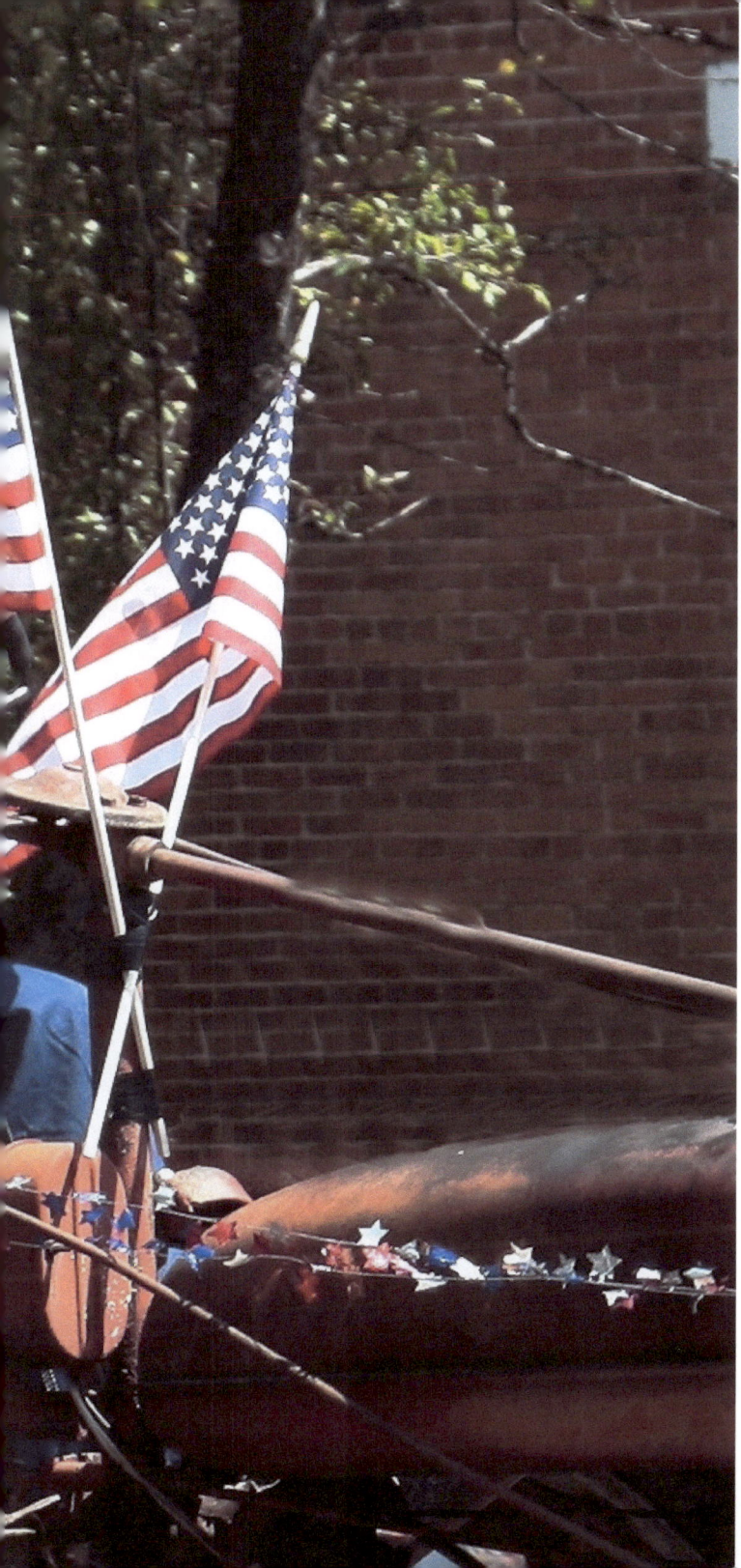

Riding With Grandpa

**July 4, 2012
Essex, NY**

Main Street becomes crowded as everyone turns out for the Spelling Bee, games, local strawberries from the Community Church, and the 4th of July Parade.

That's got to be Grandpa driving the tractor.

Lest We Forget

Essex, NY

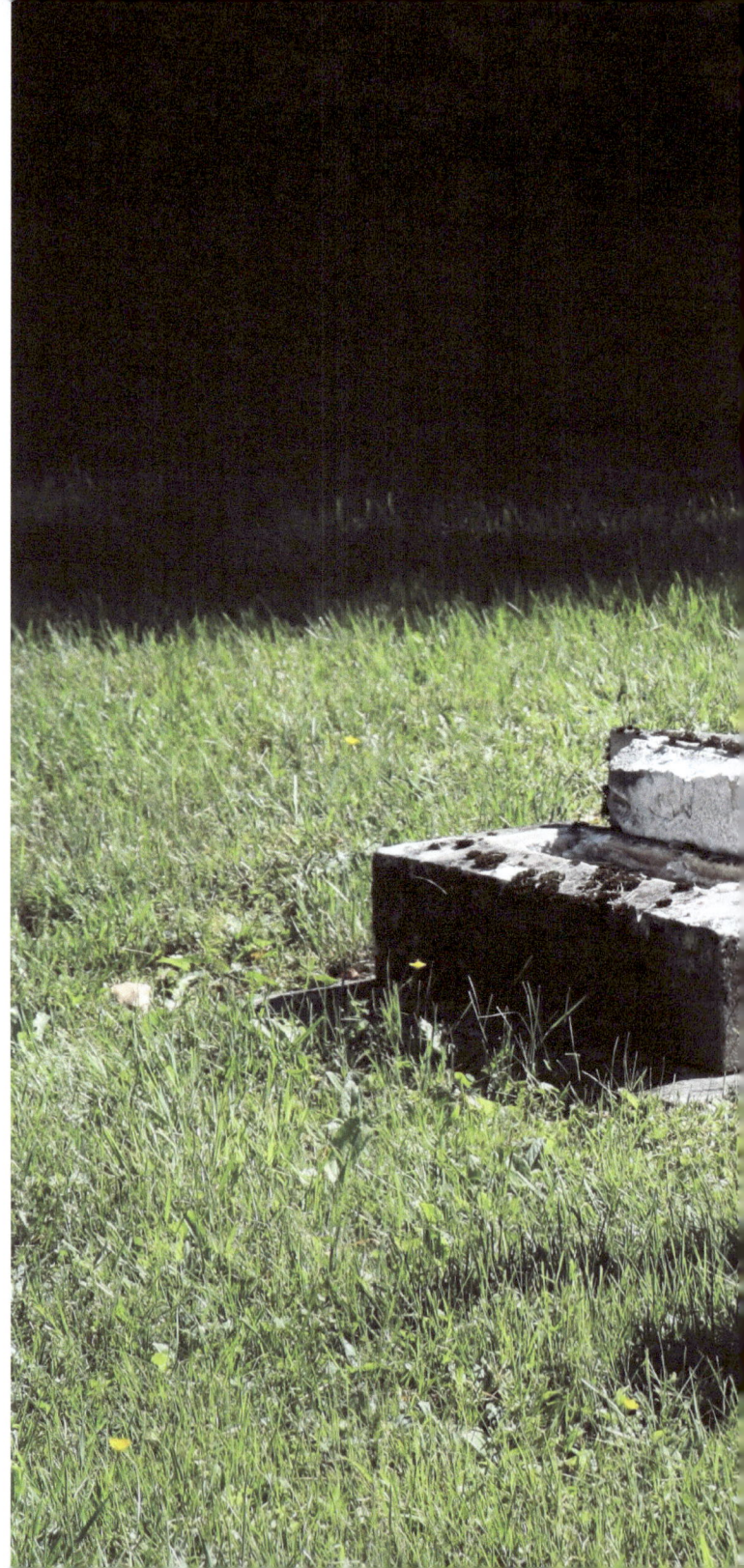

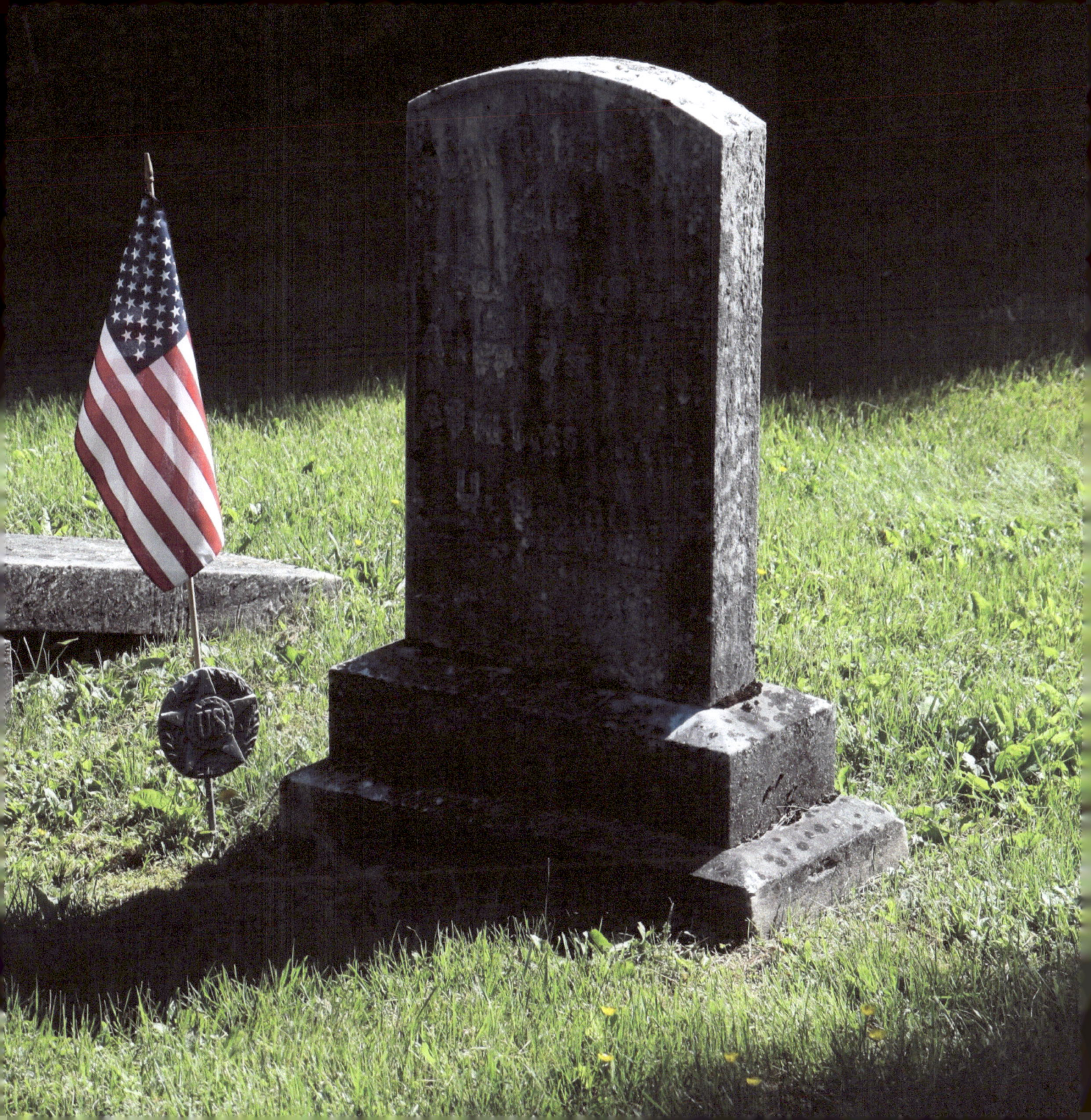

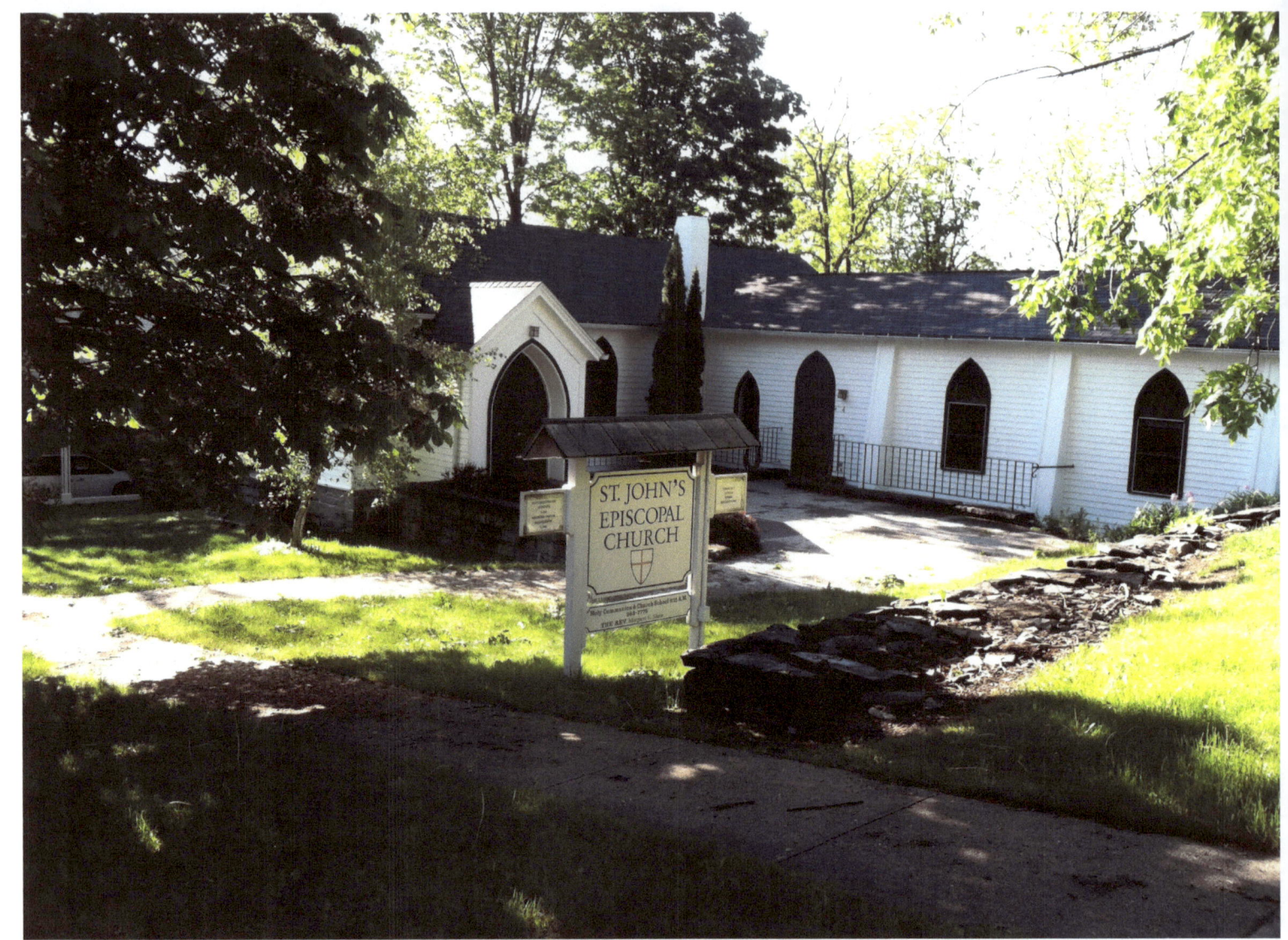

St. John's Episcopal Church

St. John's was our church away from home as well as for Anne's parents, Howard and Sara Burd Cammack. Originally built as a school for the Gilliland children (founder of Willsboro, NY), St. John's is now a charming small-town church with an active congregation. The bell tower, hidden behind the trees, contains the original school bell, now rung every Sunday.

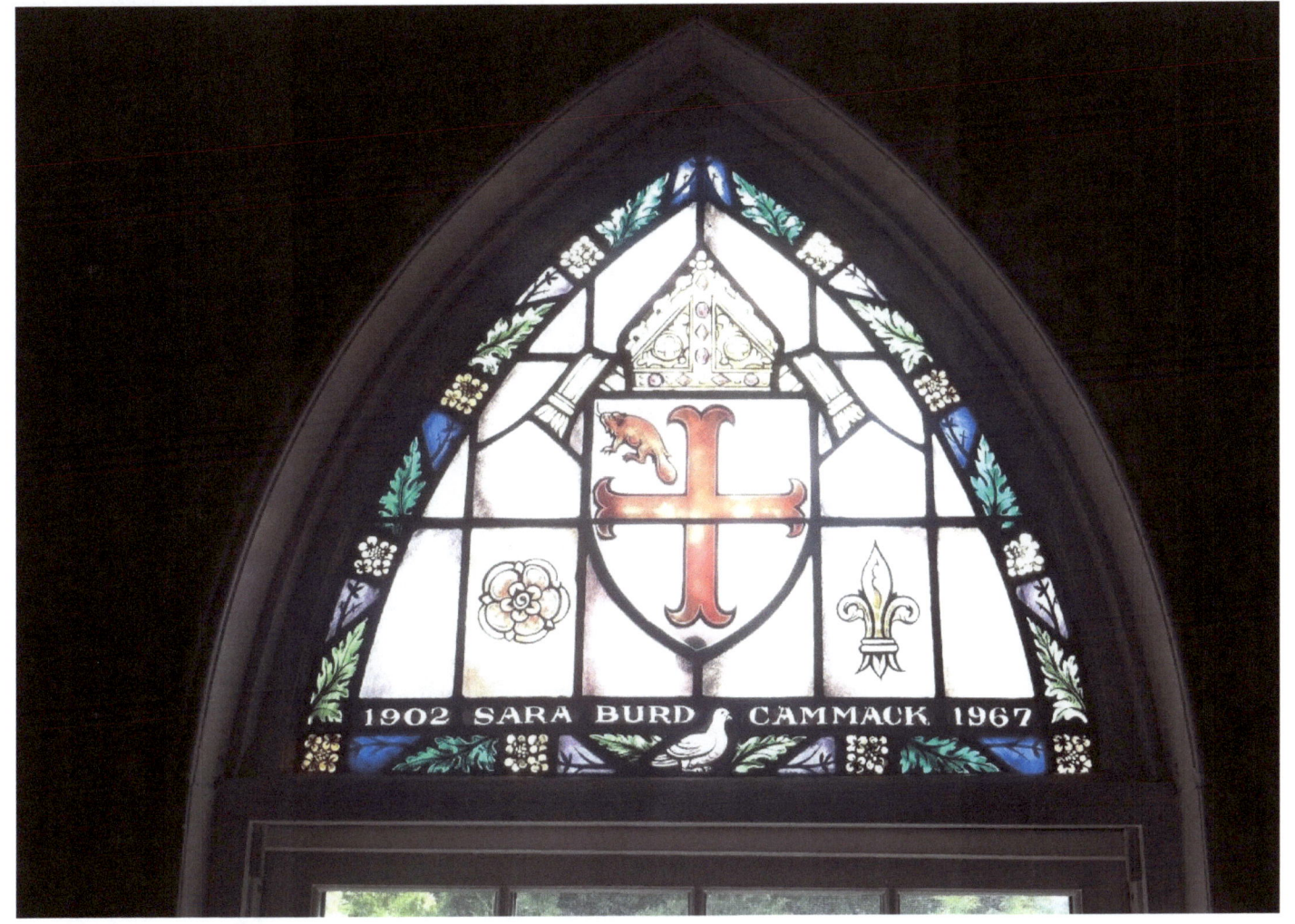

Sara Burd Cammack Window in St. John's

Stained glass window memorial to Sara Burd (Anne's mother) for her closeness to the church and the service she gave to it. Bishop Barry appointed Sara Burd President of Women for the Episcopal Diocese of Albany. During her 3-year term, she visited every parish (52). For many, this was their first visit from Albany. Mustard seeds and leaves surround the memorial window and represent growth and belief. In the center, the Seal of the Diocese of Albany (Bishop's Miter and the cross and beaver shield) represent the church she served. The Rose of Mary, on the left, is for her dedicated work with the Diocesan women, the dove is for the peace of the Holy Spirit, and the Fleur-de-lis represents the Trinity and is also a tribute to her French ancestry.

Ferry Returning to Essex

Taken from the Old Dock Inn, Essex, NY

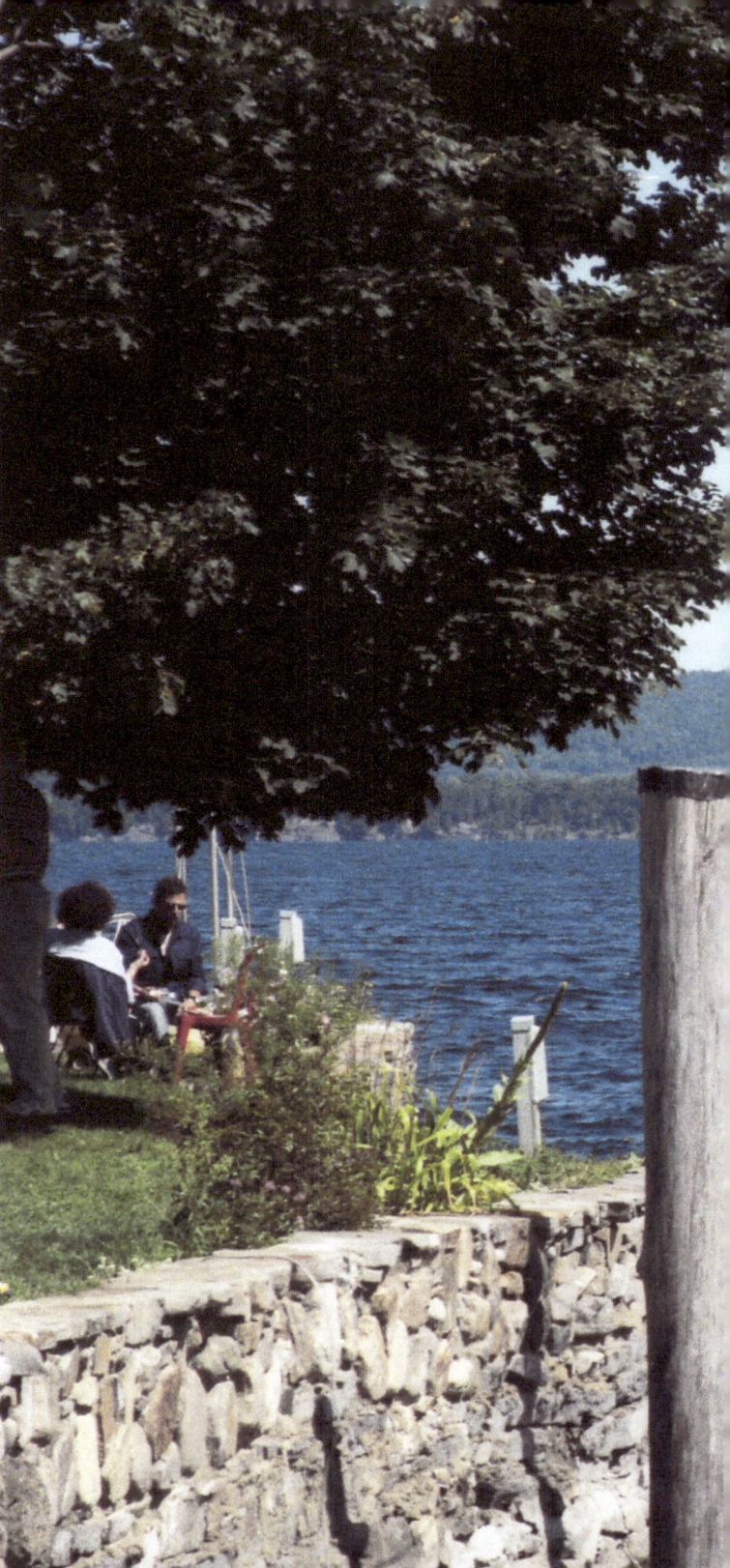

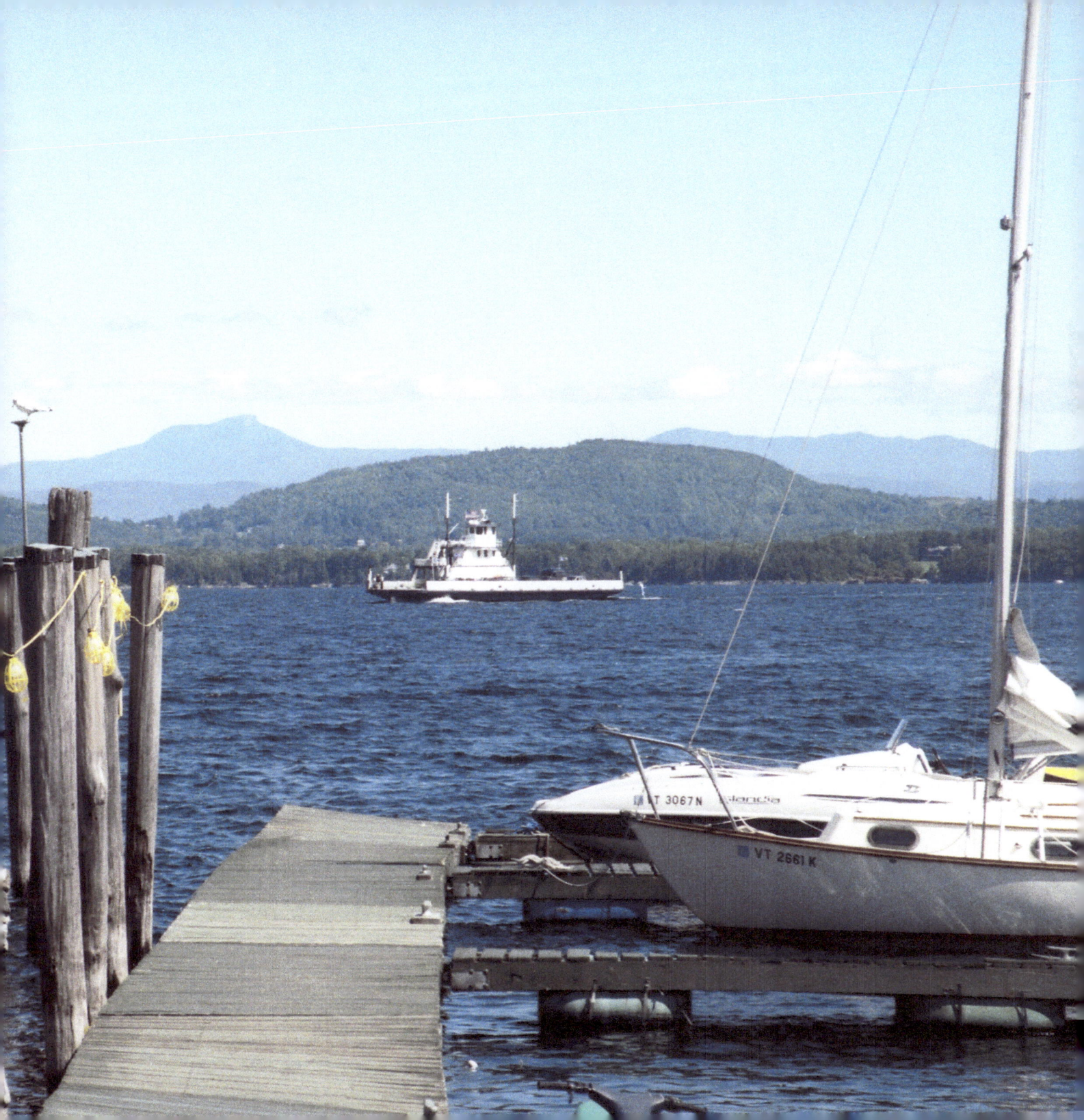

Sailing on Lake Champlain

Lake Champlain is the largest body of fresh water in the country, after the Great Lakes. During the Colonial Era, Lake Champlain, at 125 miles in length, was part of the principle transportation route from New York City to Quebec, Canada. As a result, the lake was the scene of several naval battles during the Revolutionary War and the War of 1812 which took place in the same areas that we sailed each summer.

The lake is 3 miles across at our waterfront, is 400' deep off Split Rock, and provided us some of the most interesting and exciting sailing available on the lake.

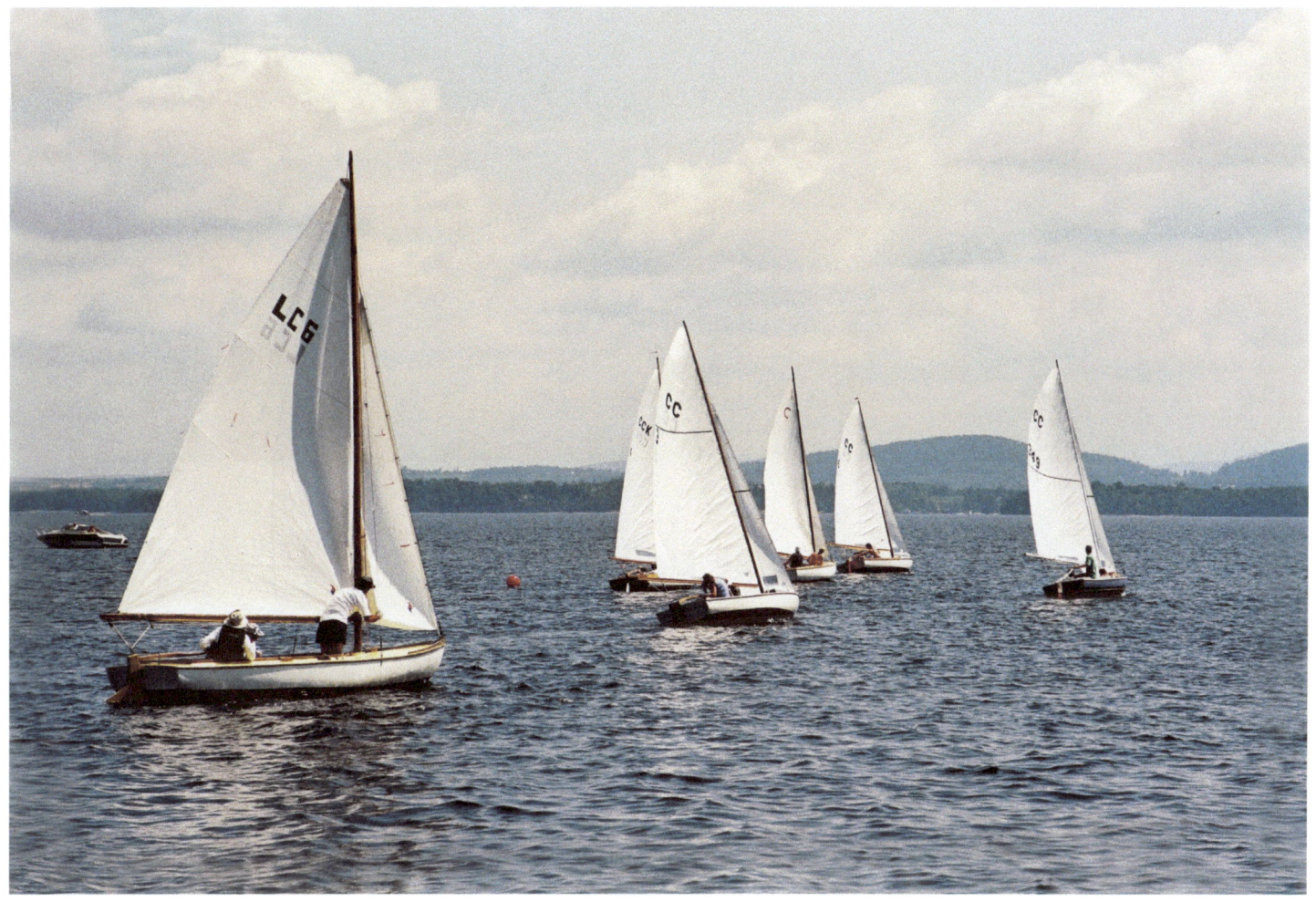

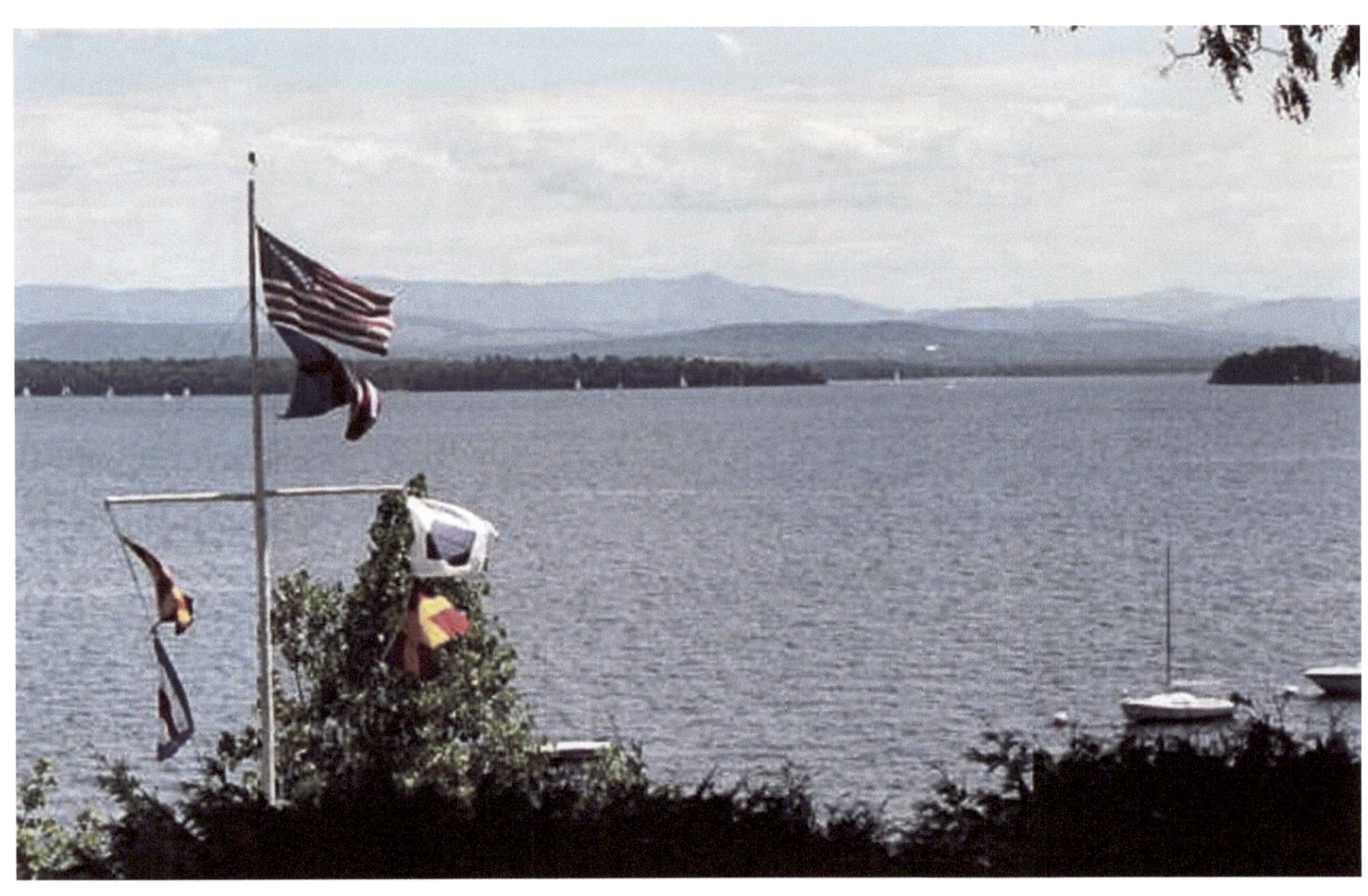

Race Day Flags

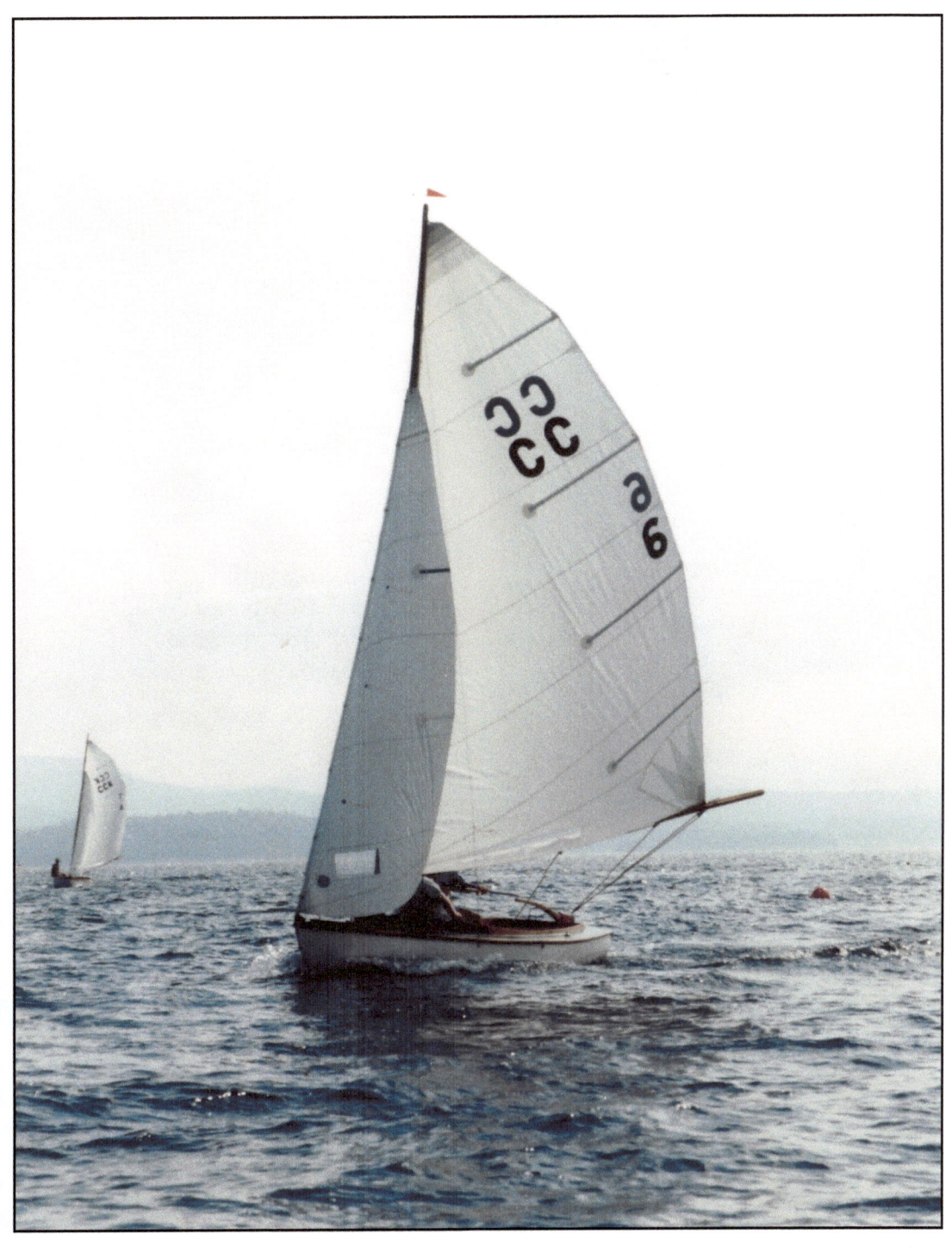

Valcour in the lead

Cape Cod Knockabouts from the Split Rock Yacht Club raced on Saturday mornings.

Valcour was our knockabout for several years until we purchased Arcturus, a Tanzer 22.

This photo was taken when Ken Grillo was Valcour's owner.

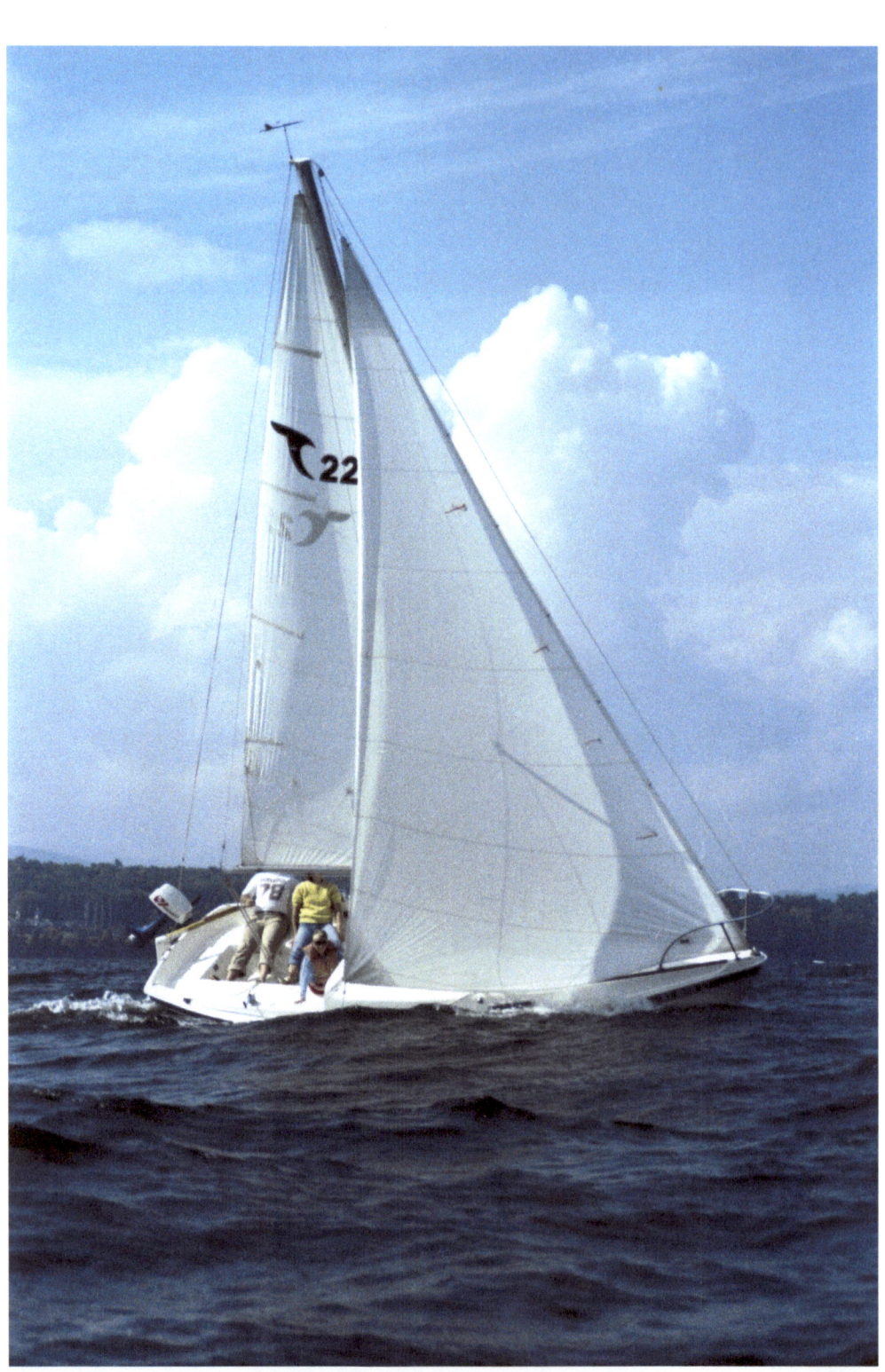

Underway in Arcturus

A brisk sailing day on Lake Champlain.

Arcturus is under full sail and making hull speed with her leeward gunwale awash.

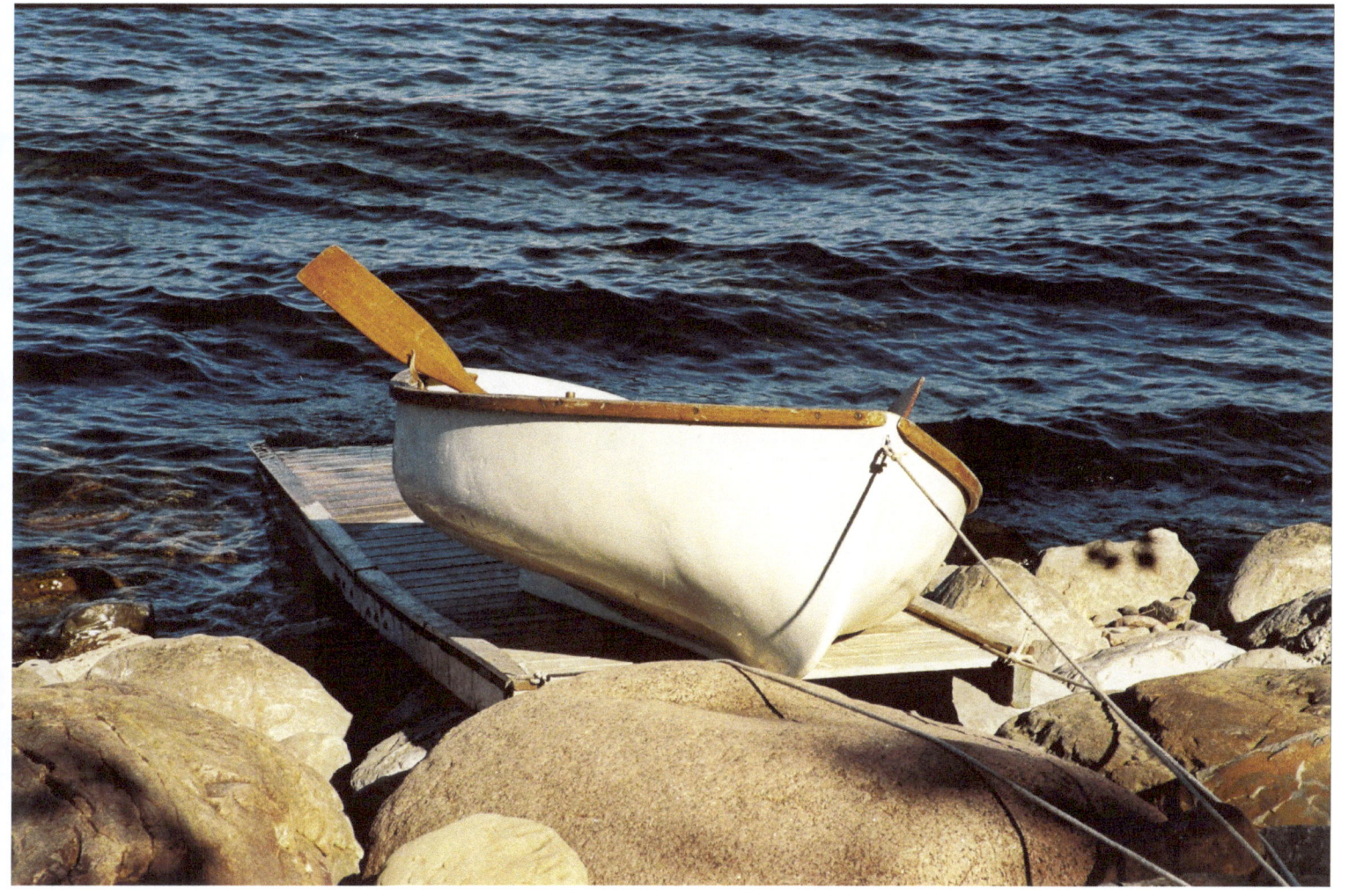

Ready to Go

It was mid-afternoon of a dry summer day with a lovely south wind blowing, I thought I should get a picture of the dinghy we'd just built before it became scarred with use. We made this dinghy in the basement of our Slingerlands house after expanding the line drawings found in a tiny business card size ad in Yachting Magazine.

The dinghy got us out and back to Valcour and the Plastic Wood for years. During a busy summer the Crater Club waterfront would be covered with sunfish and dinghies on boat slides like this.

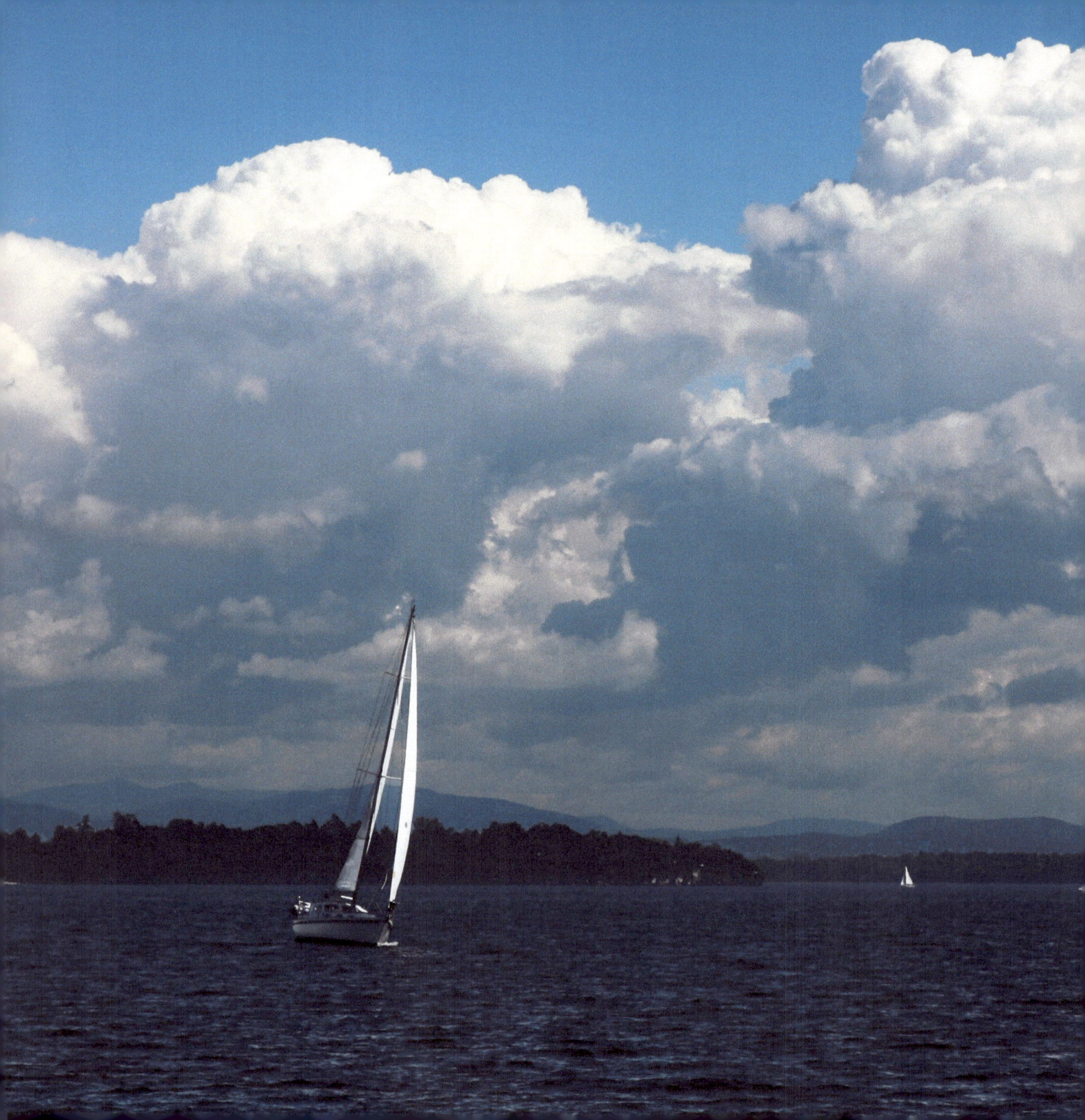

Sailboat crossing Thompson's Point

A fun family outing on Lake Champlain was to sail across to Vermont, anchor behind Gardner Island, swim off the boat, eat a picnic lunch on board, and then sail back.

On the sail back to NY, we might troll for Champy, Lake Champlain's own sea monster, which always gave the grandkids a thrill.

In spite of our best efforts and the top quality bait we used, we never got a nibble.

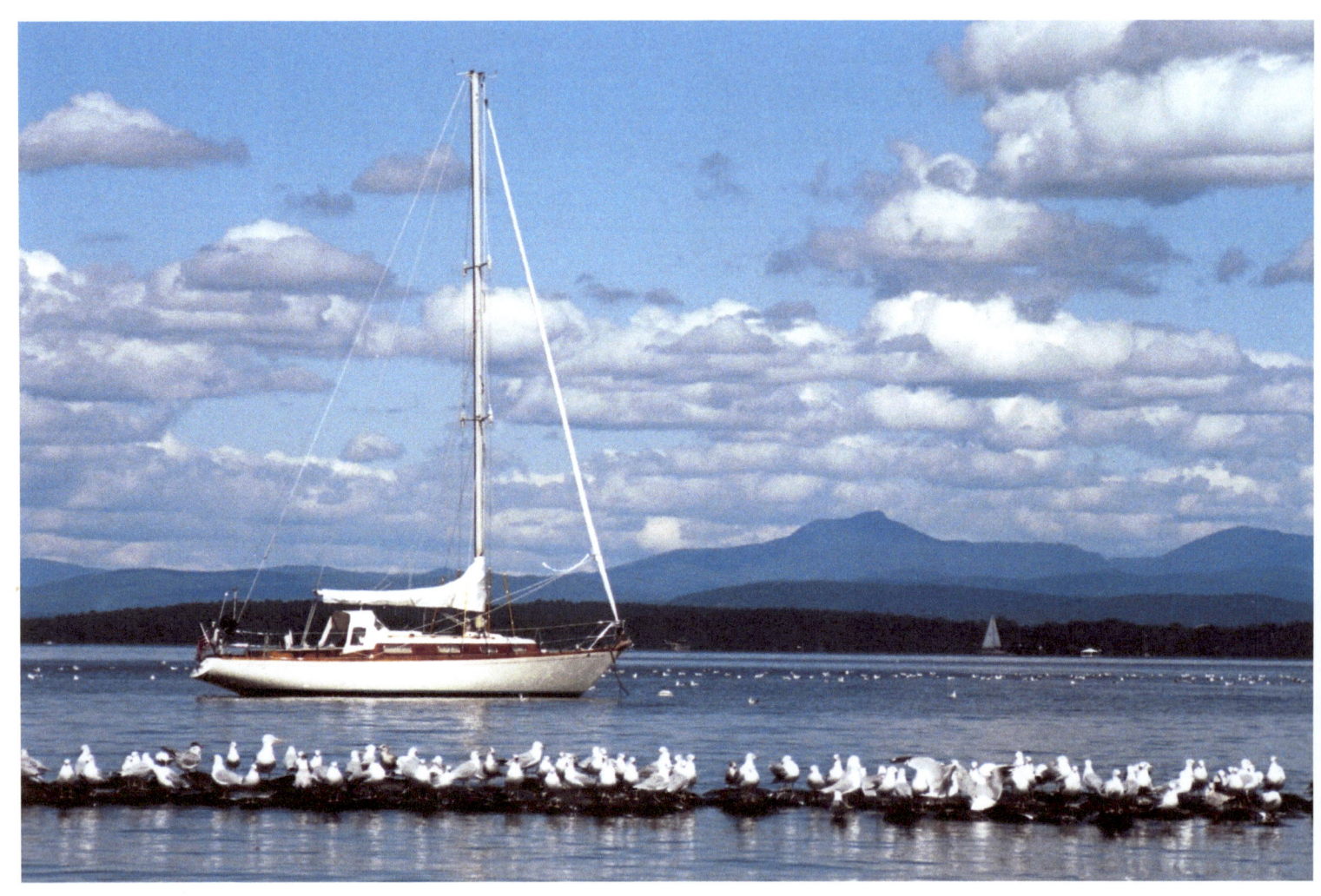

Camel's Hump from Westport
Westport Yacht Club, Westport, NY

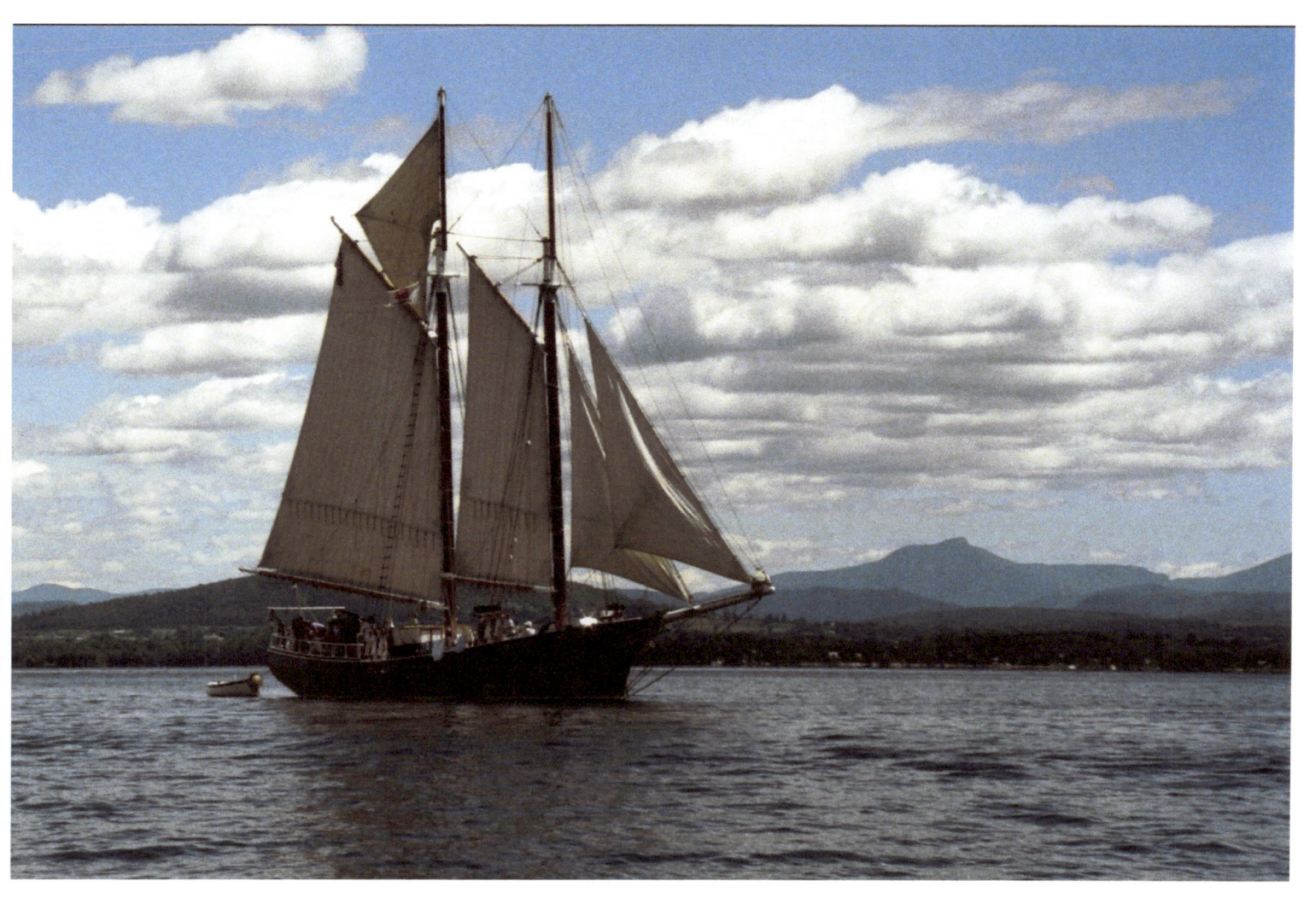

Homer Dixon on Lake Champlain

Adirondack Beauty

The Adirondack Mountains are incredibly beautiful and I have been privileged to have both enjoyed and photographed them in their glory.

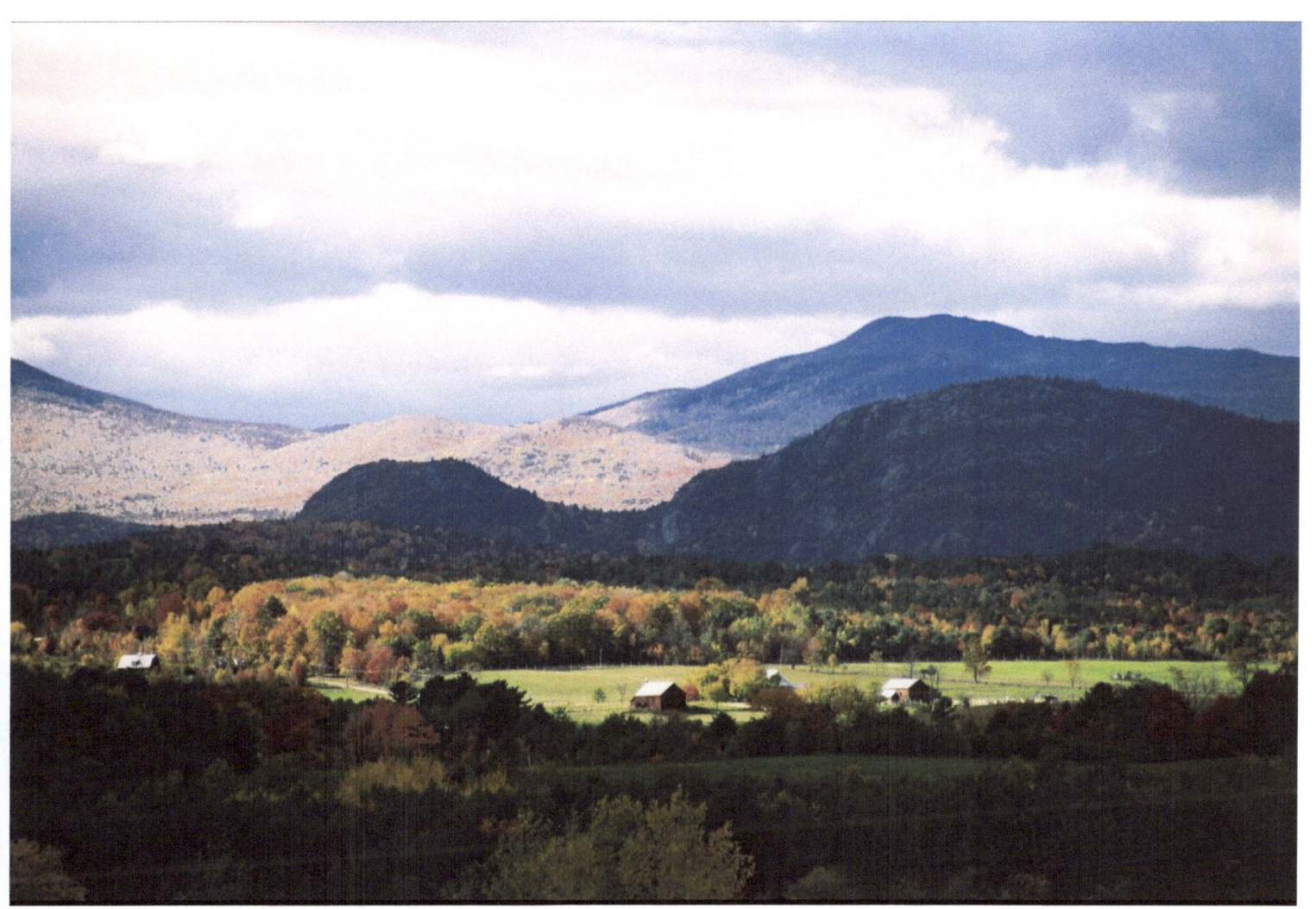

Behind Westport

Ausable River

The Ausable is a 94 mile river that flows through the Adirondack Mountains past the village of Lake Placid and empties into Lake Champlain.

It was originally named "Au Sable" (French for "of sand") by Samuel de Champlain when he explored the region in 1609 because of its extensive sandy delta.

The Ausable River is known for its spectacular gorge, Ausable Chasm, as well as being one of the best trout rivers in the eastern USA.

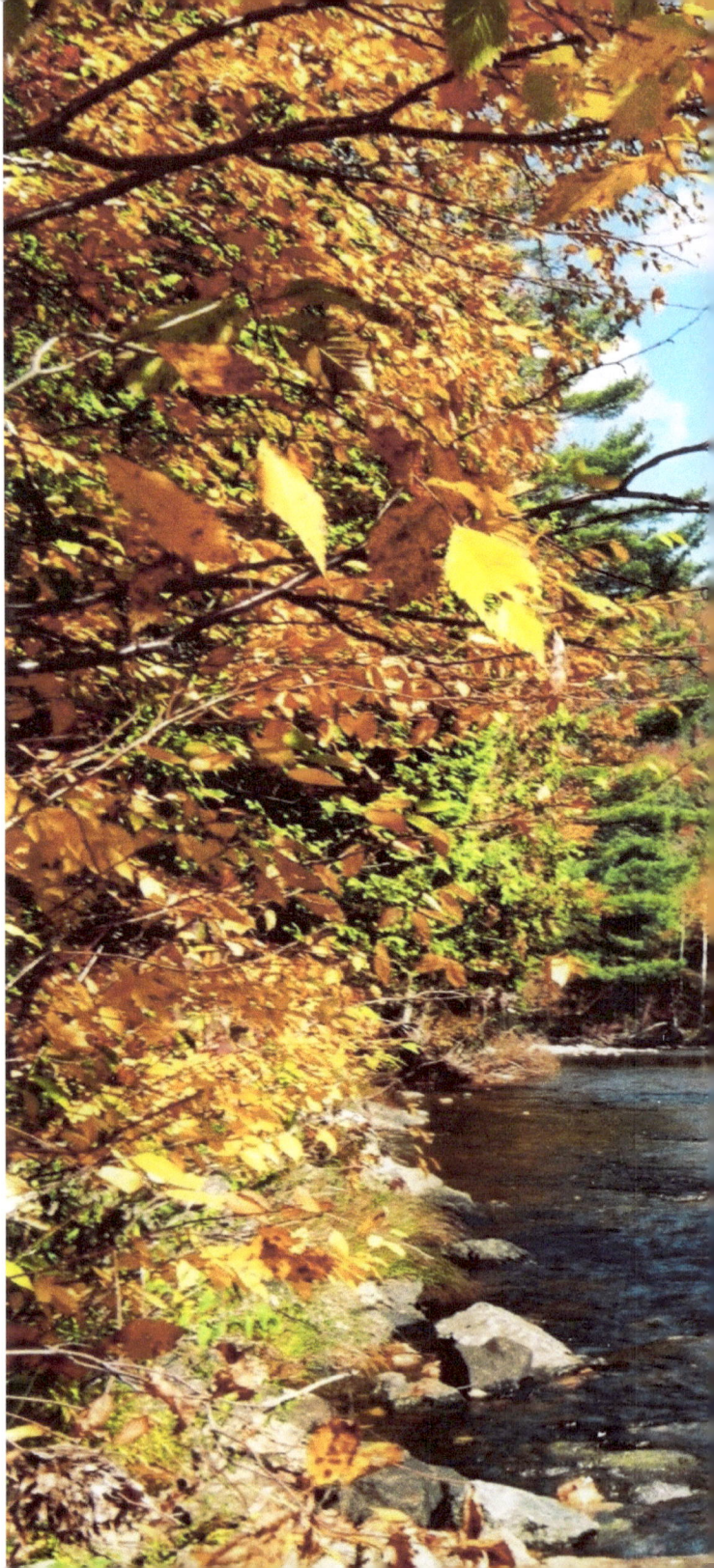

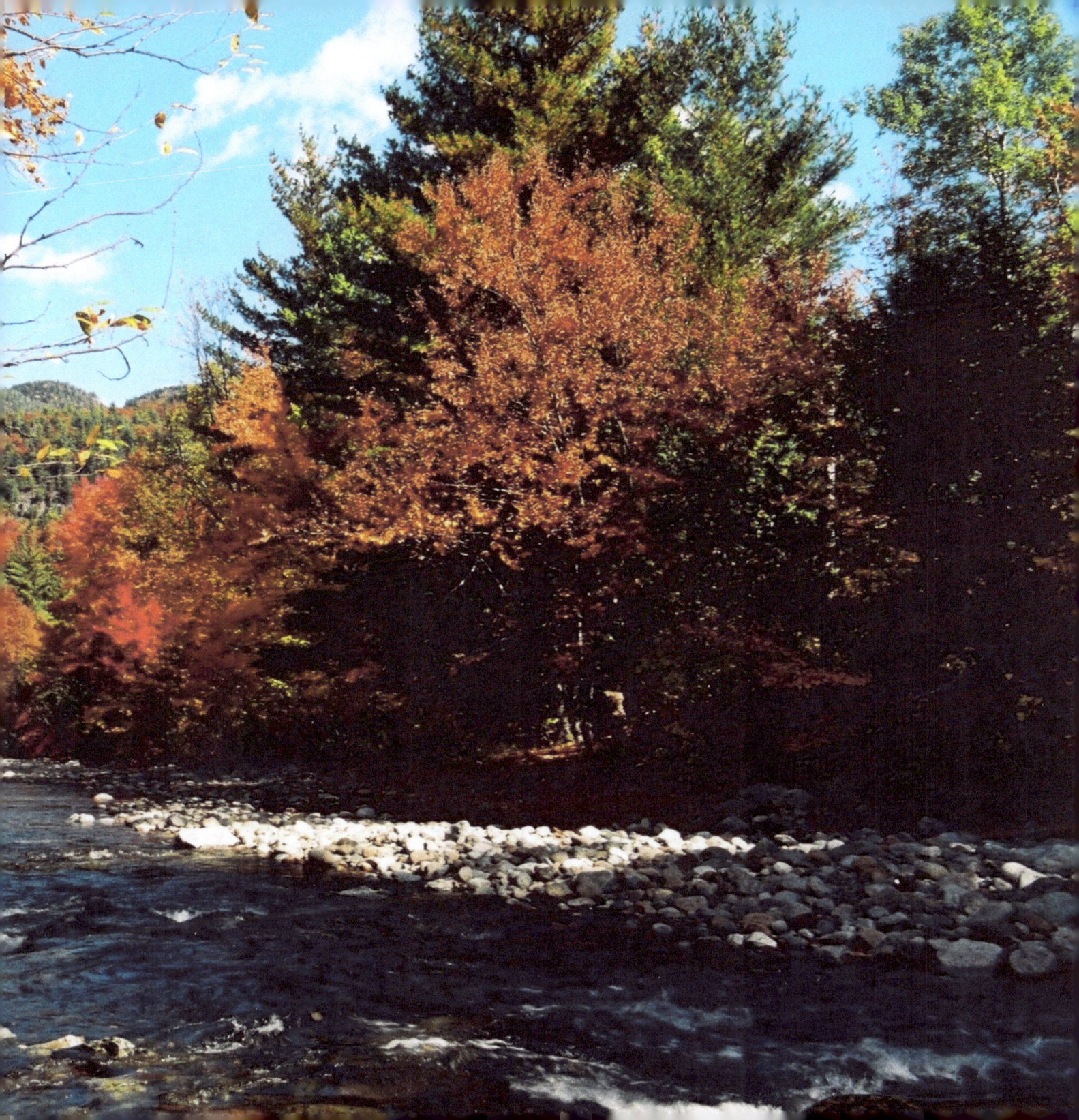

Falls on the Ausable River

Jay, NY

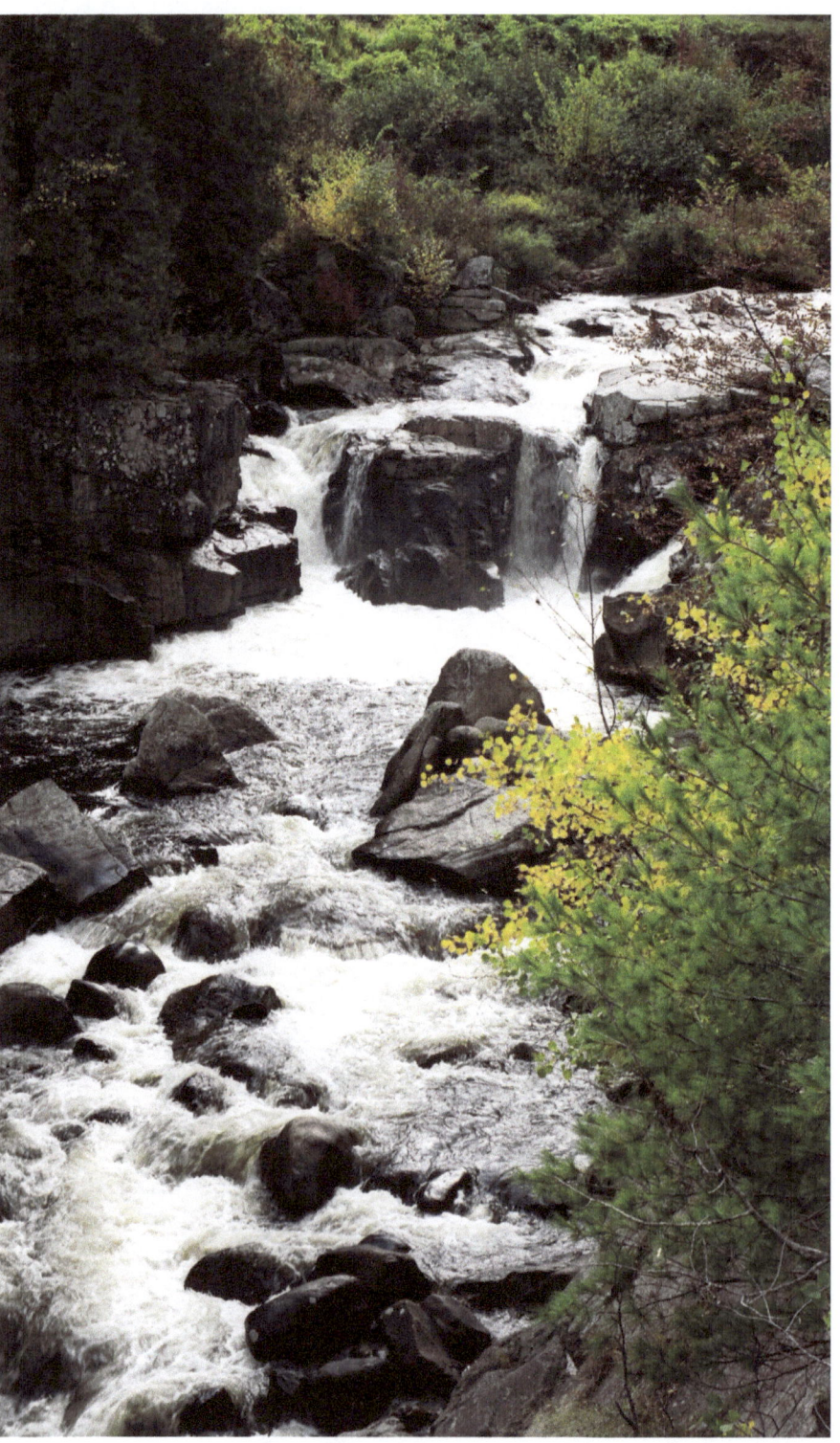

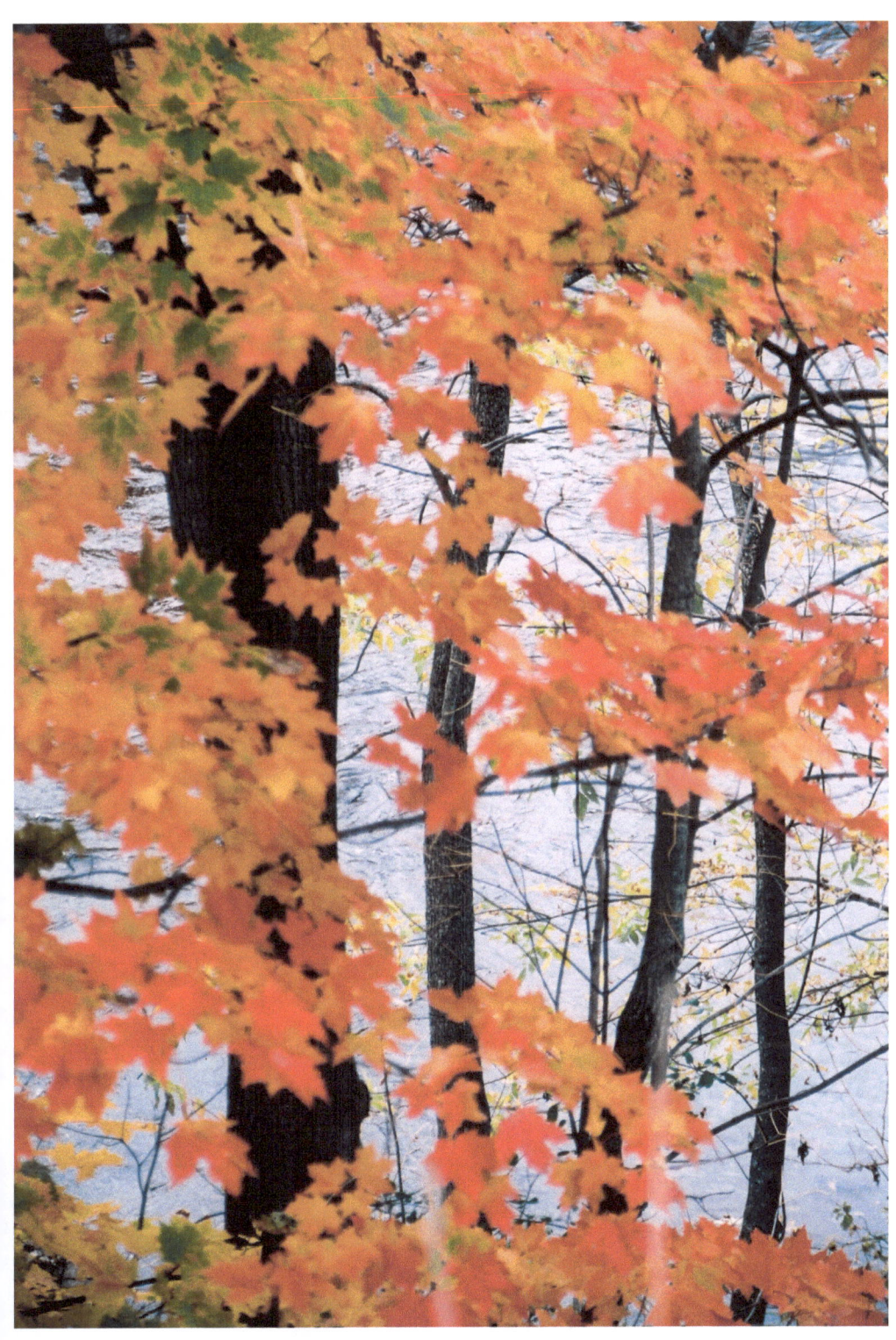

Boquet River Side

Whallonsburg, NY

The fall coloring around Essex was outstanding this year and by walking along the Boquet River looking for good photo opportunities, I got this one.

High Peaks with Chickory

Giant Mountain is easily identified by its rockslide scarred face.

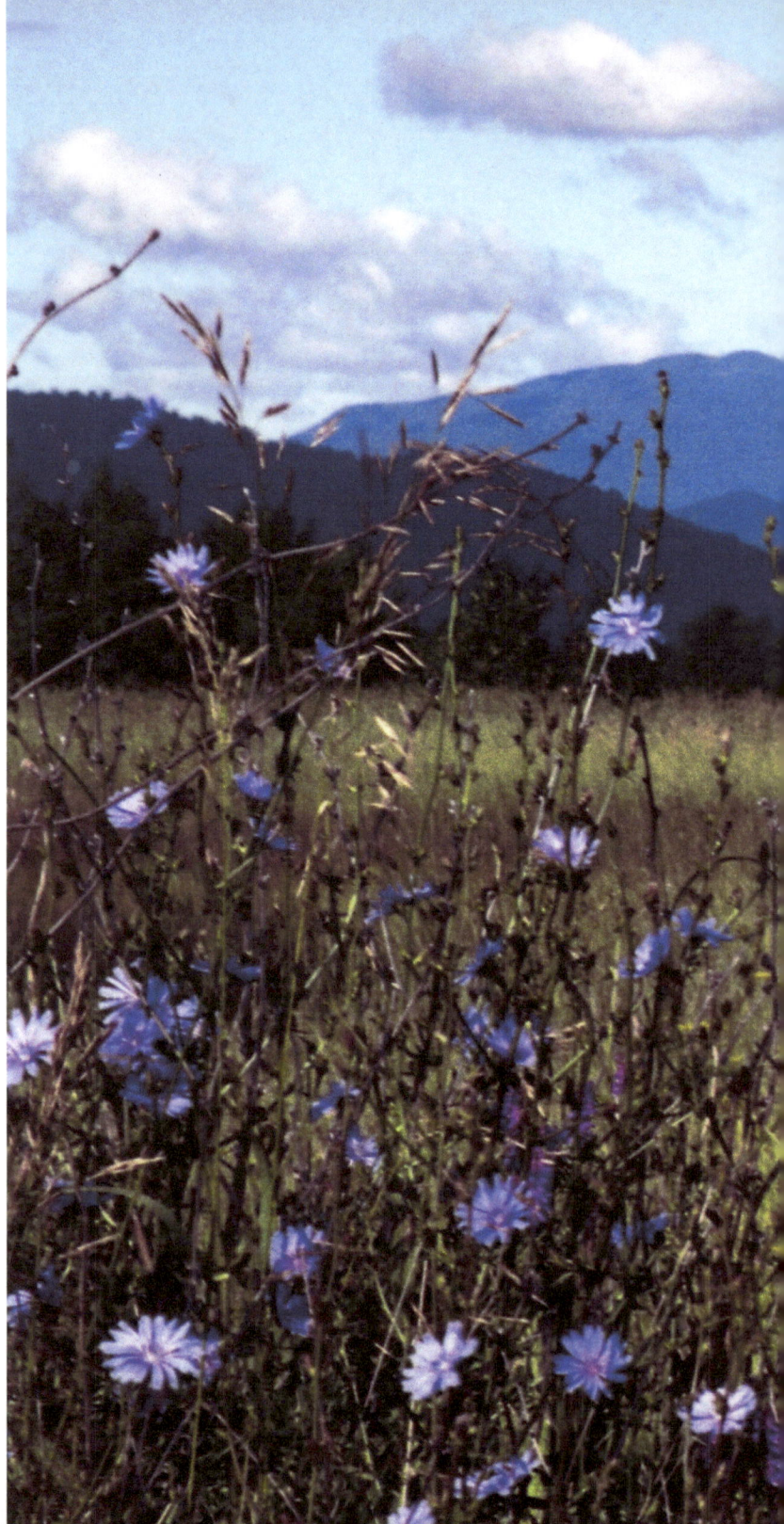

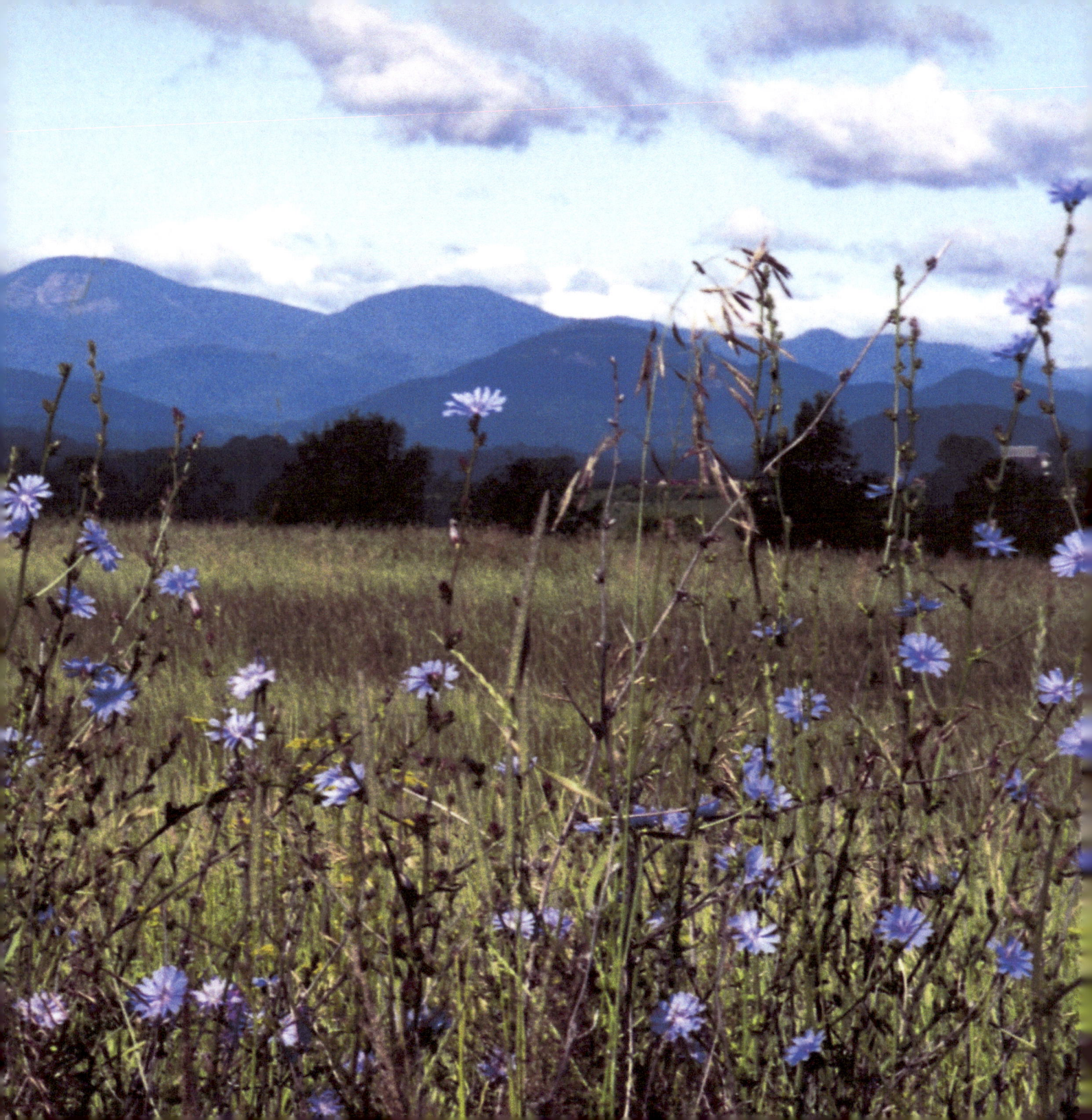

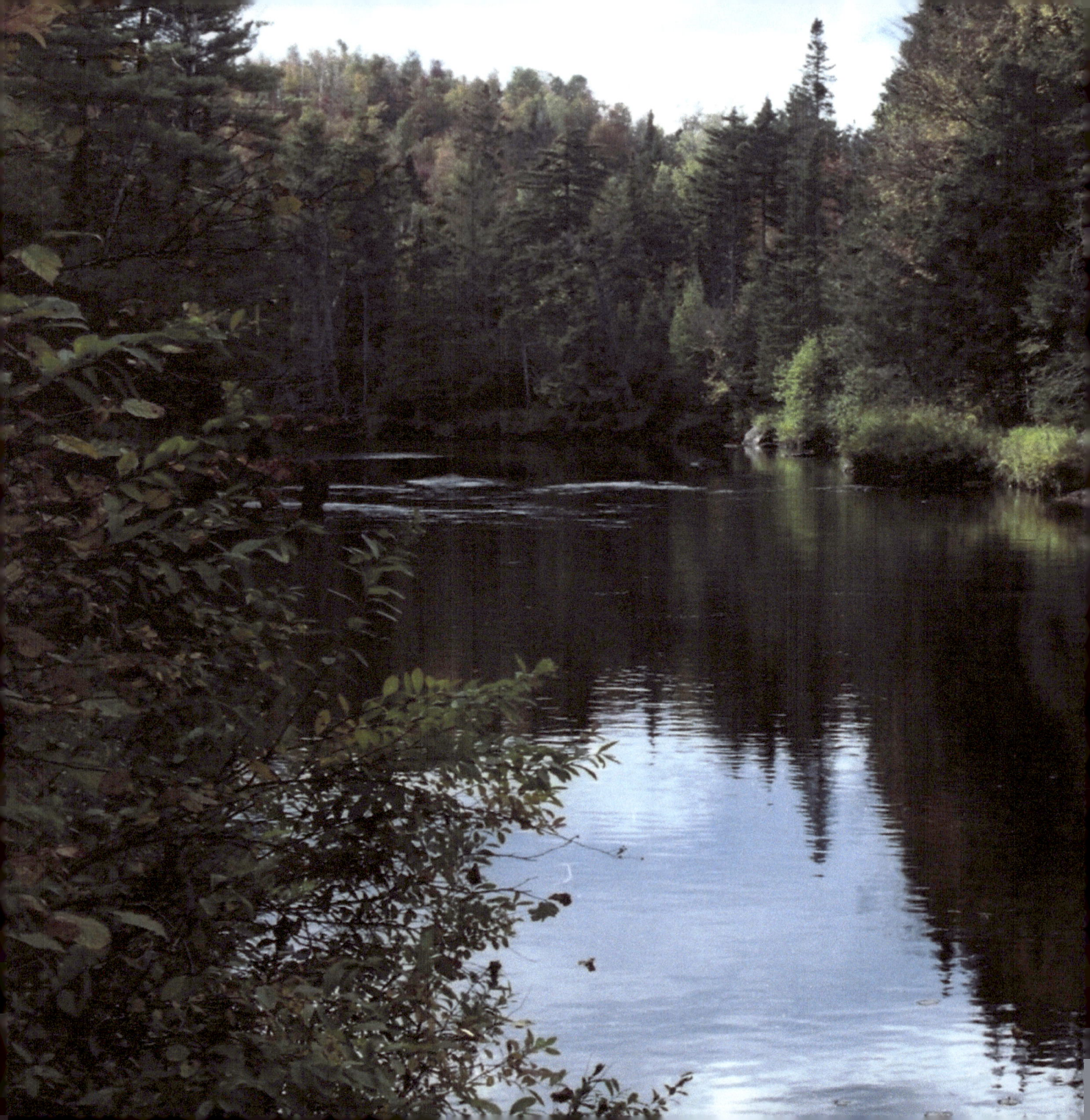

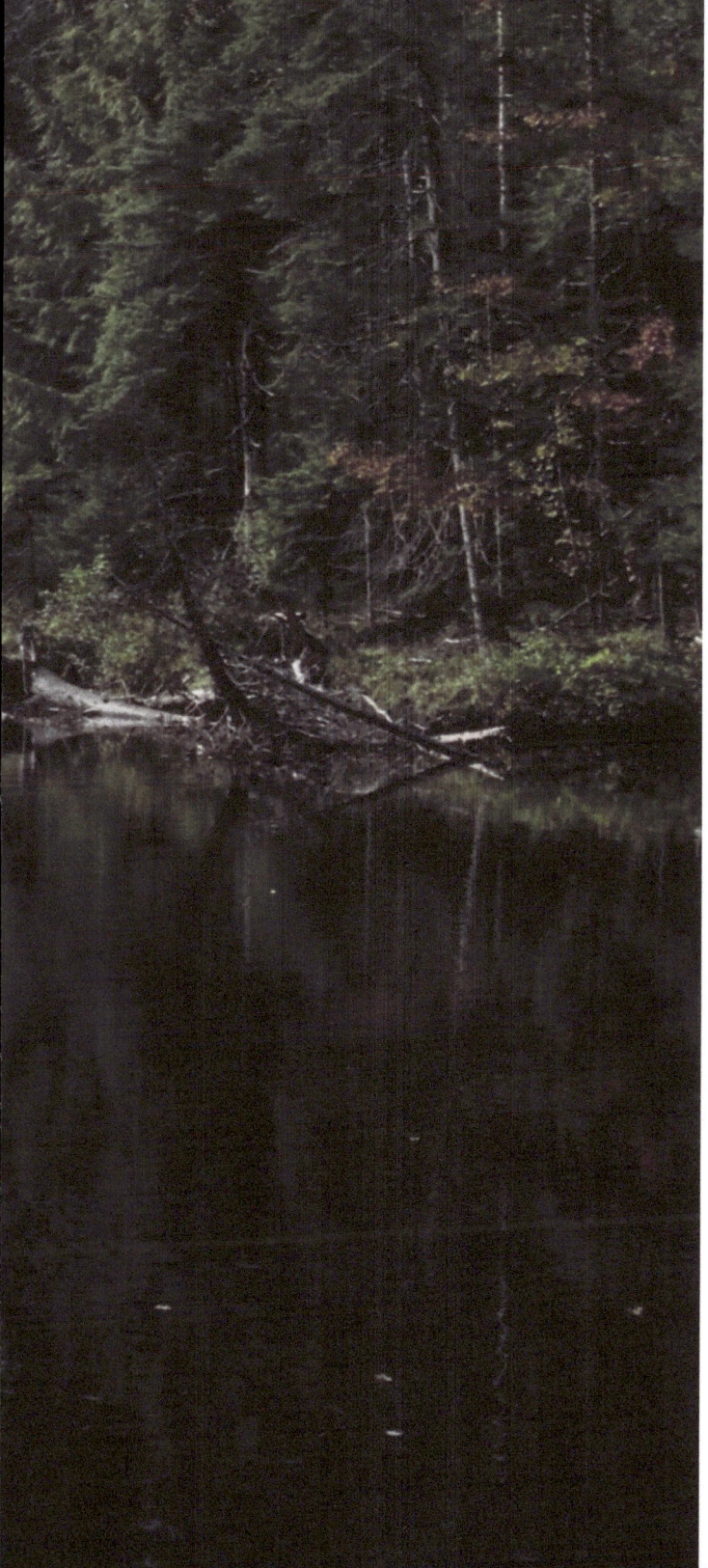

Ausable River

Near Whiteface, NY

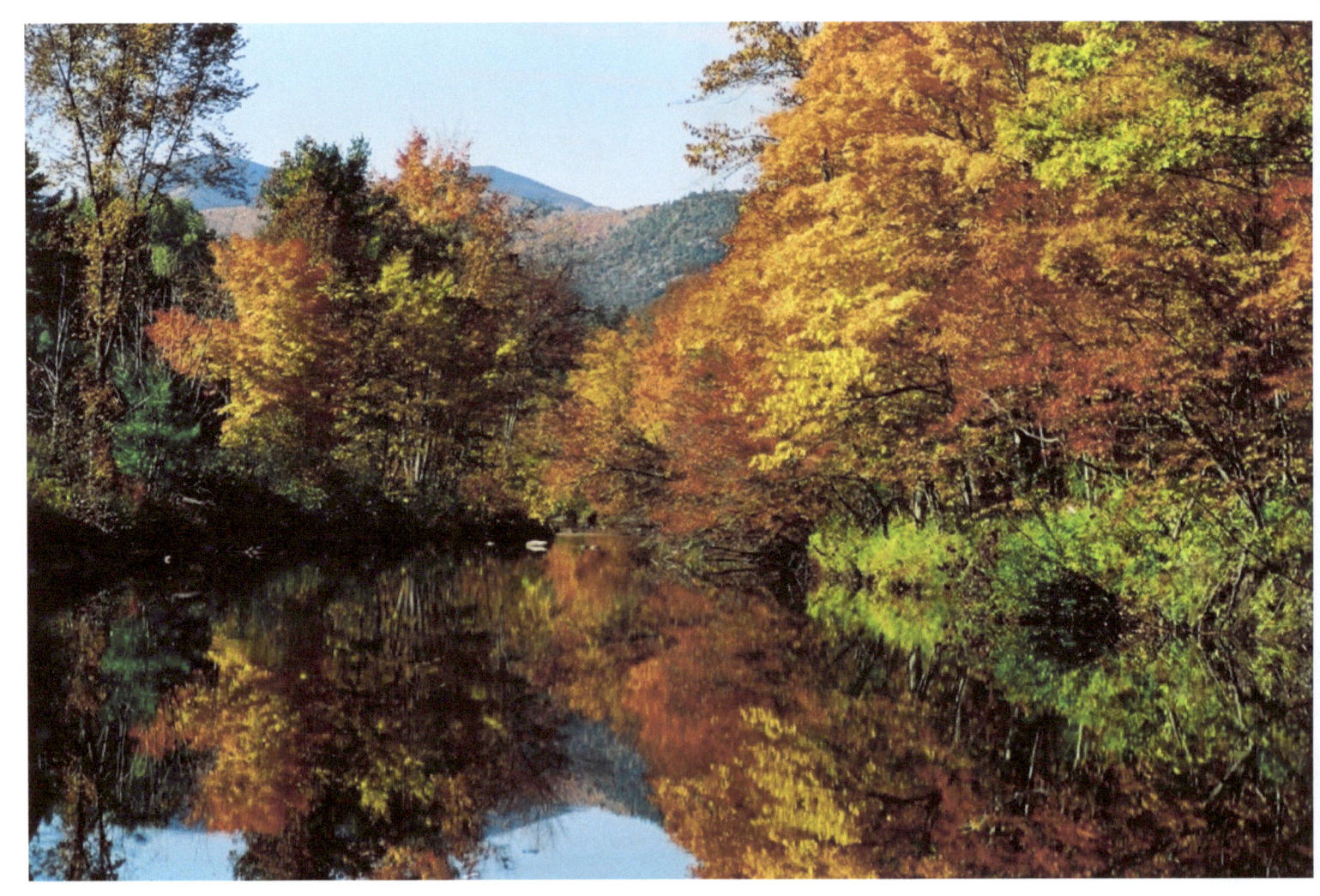

Fall Reflections

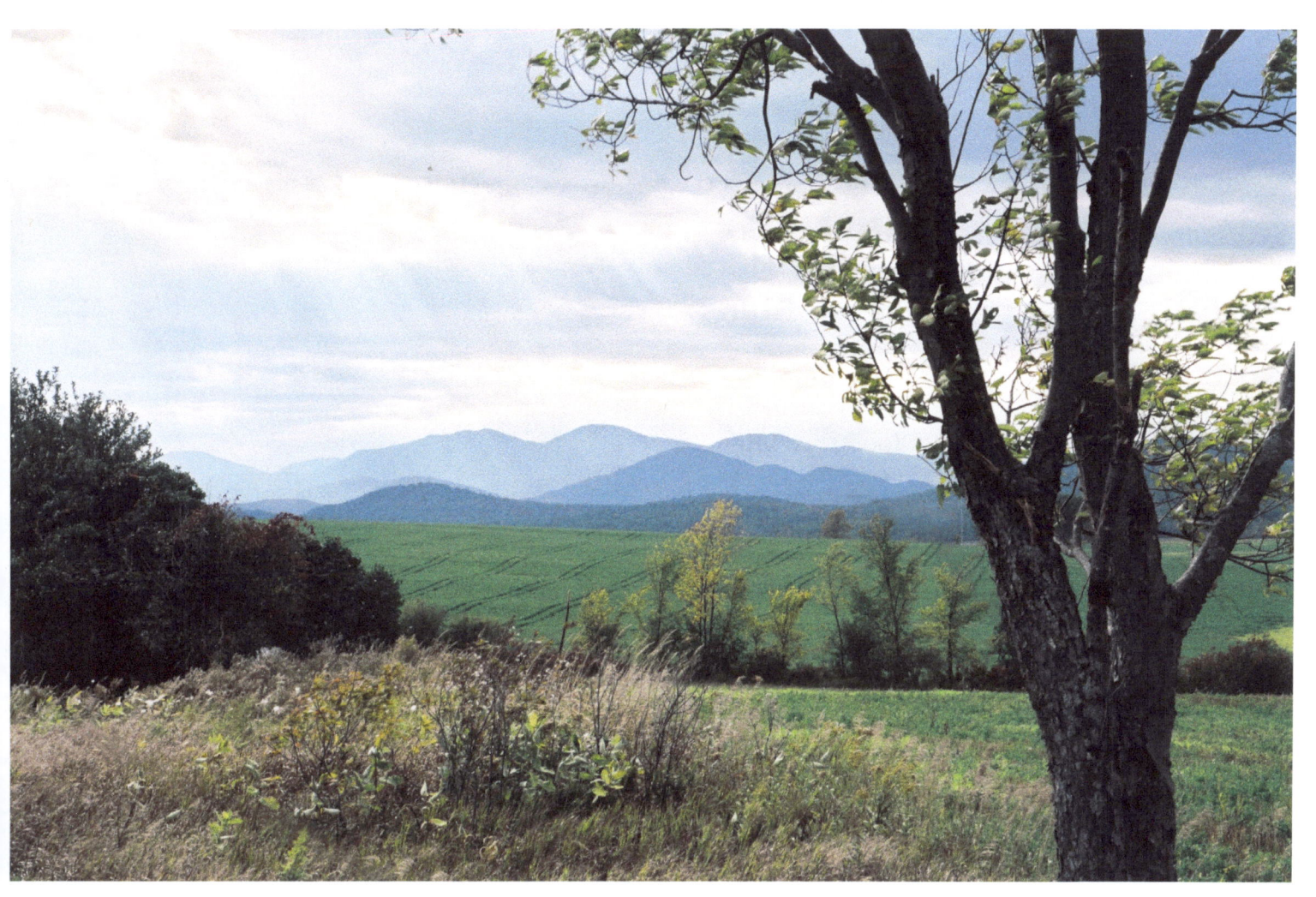

Adirondack High Peaks from Whallonsburg

Adirondacks from the Ausable Club

Ausable, NY

I took this while standing in front of the Ausable Club building.

This could well have been taken the same glorious fall as the Boquet River Side photograph.

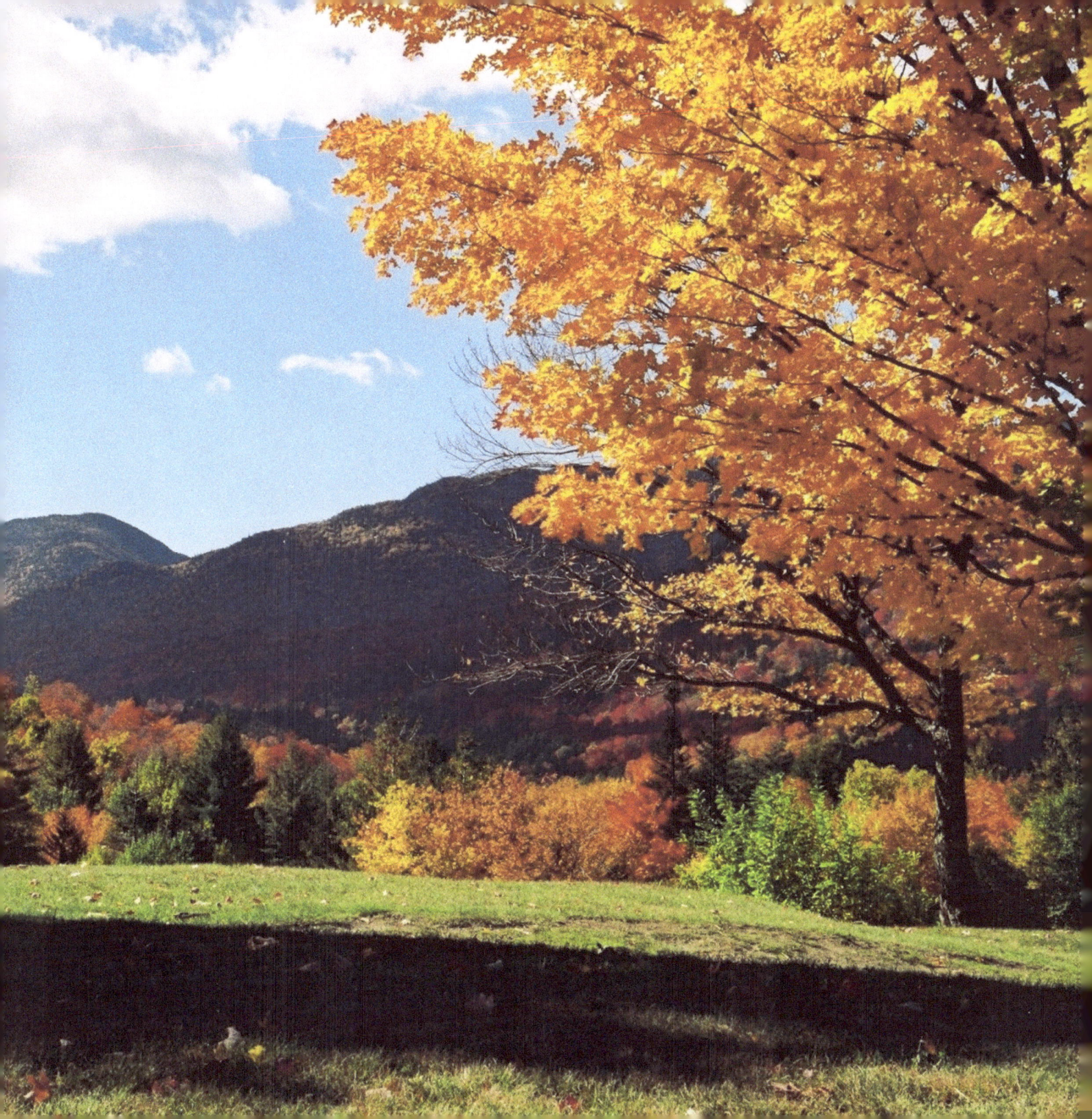

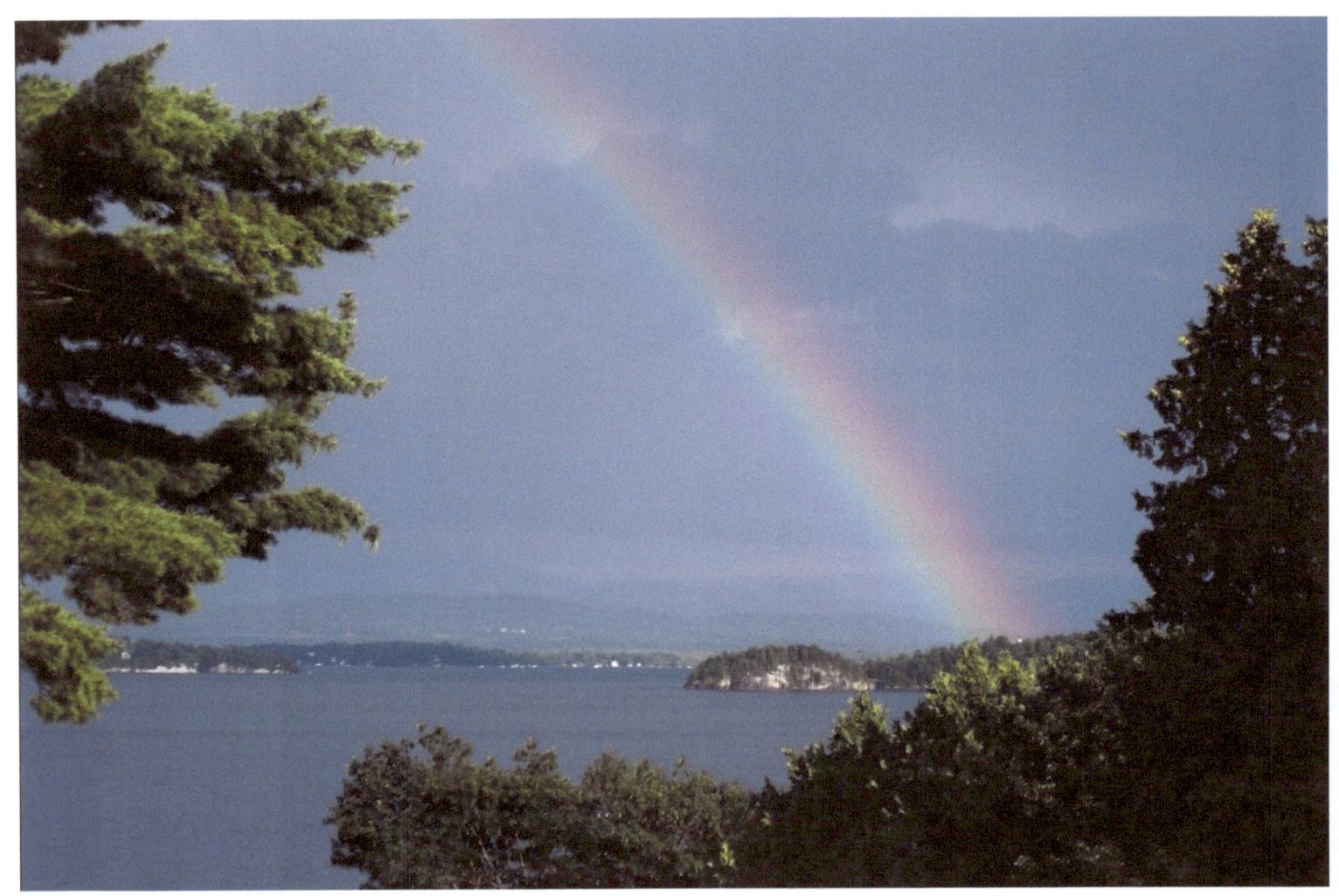

Rainbow Over Split Rock
Essex, NY

Taken from the porch of Captain's Cabin.

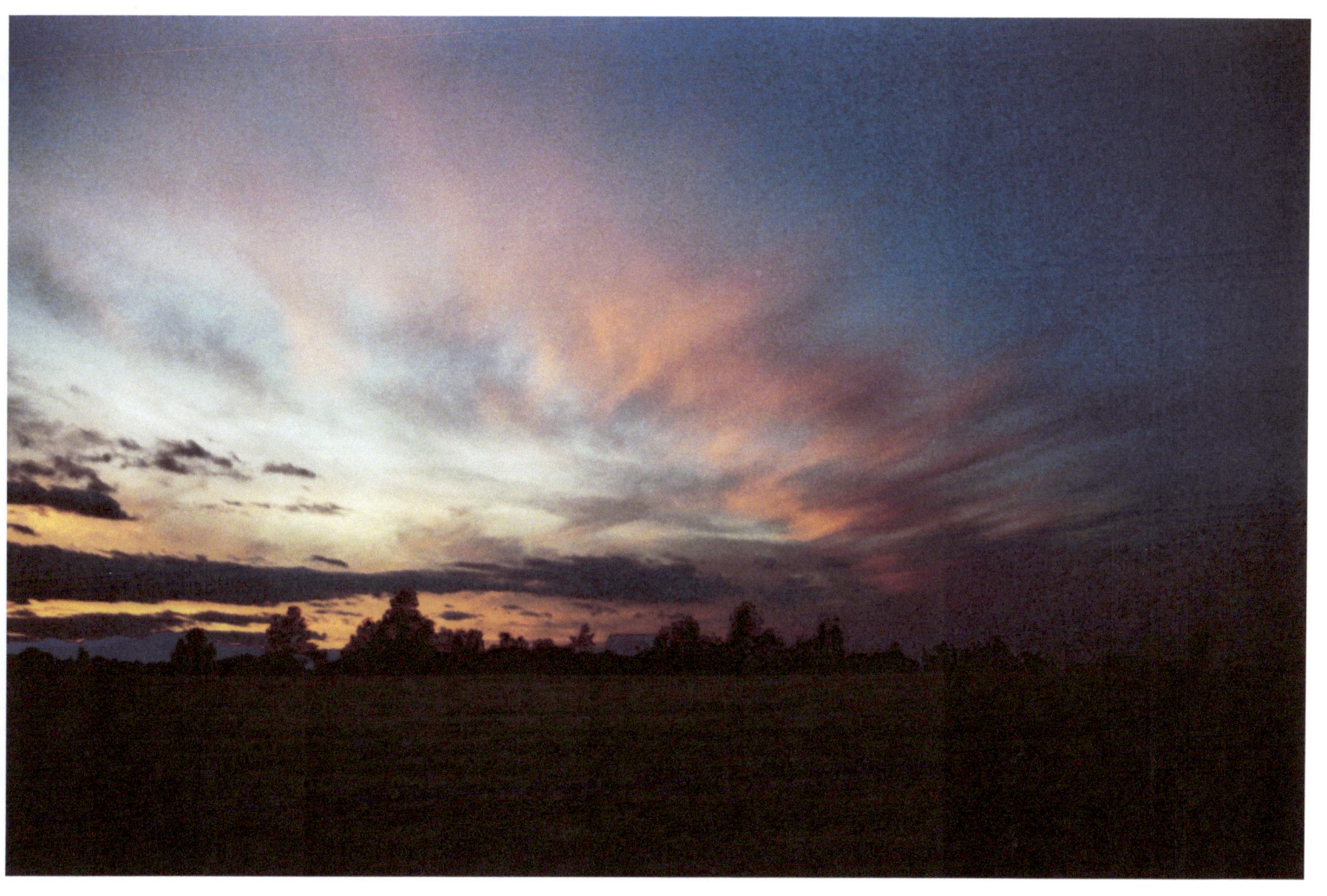

Sunset
Essex, NY

Stand Easy became our art gallery as we framed and hung the photographs we liked on its walls. From its perch over the phone table, *Sunset* graced the great room.

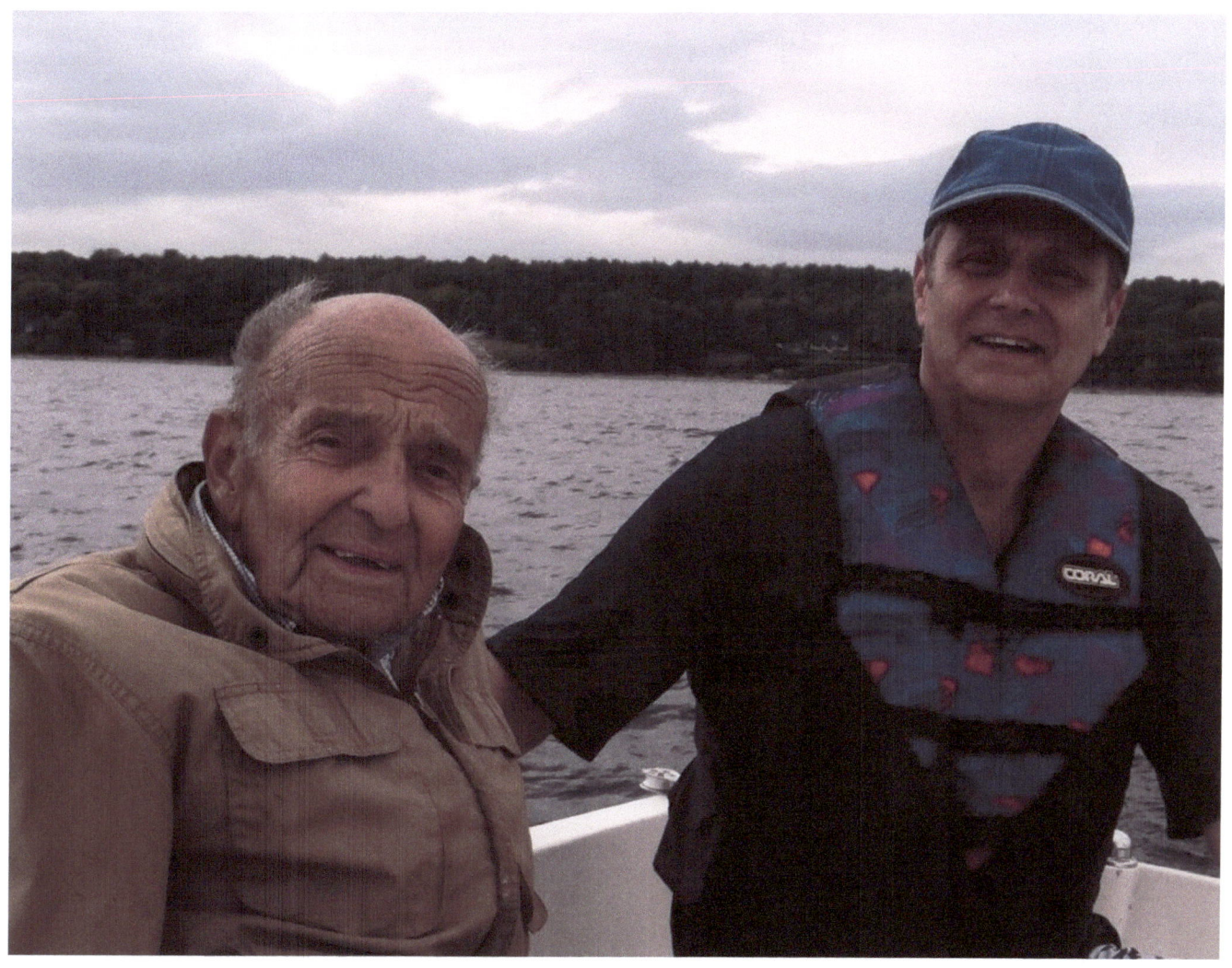

Benjamin Yates Brewster Jr., and his son James Burd Brewster enjoying their absolutely favoritest activity; sailing on Lake Champlain in Arcturus, Ben and Anne's sailboat.

Ben as a boy learned to sail on Lake Sebago in Sebago, ME., while attending Camp O-At-Ka and as an adult taught all of his children to sail on Lake Champlain while summering at the Crater Club in Essex, NY.